NAKED!
Womanizer
Awaken Your Inner Rebel

For Every
Woman Who
Dares to
Dream Bigger

by

The
Red Heel BOSS

ISBN: 978-1-966798-81-1

To my daughters — my why — who remind me daily what strength looks like.

To every woman ready to live unapologetically and reclaim her power.

Table of Contents

Acknowledgment

To my daughters—you are my heart, my why, and my forever reminder that we lead by example, not perfection. You've seen me fall, rebuild, and rise—and still, you choose to love me in every version. This book is as much yours as it is mine.

To my family including my work family and closest, truest friends—thank you for the steady love, for holding space for my fire, even when it got messy. For the tears and the laughs, the grounding, the chats and the calls, and the shoulders I leaned on when I forgot how strong I was.

To the ones who challenged me, doubted me, betrayed me, or tried to shrink me—thank you. You were the fire that burned away everything I no longer needed to carry. Every heartbreak, every storm, every dark night cracked me open to my own light. You helped me grow—some of you without even realizing it. Thank you for being the mirror and the match.

To the women I've worked with, connected with, and to you—reading this now:

You were never broken—only doubted.

This book is for you:

For the woman tired of just surviving.

For the woman ready to rise, to earn, and to live on her own terms.

For the one who knows, deep in her bones, she's meant for more—

More freedom.

More fulfillment.

More financial power.

This book is a tribute to free will, truth, rebellion, and every woman daring to own her story—unfiltered and unapologetic.

This is where healing begins. And building, too.

A business. A brand. A life. *YOU.*

From the inside out. Unapologetically. Because you matter.

Let this be your permission slip to want it all—and go get it.

This is more than gratitude—it's a celebration of the women who choose to live NAKED! in the truest sense: unfiltered, unbound, and unafraid to rise.

Reclaiming Our True Selves – A Journey to Freedom

NAKED! is the symbol of your power reclaimed by stripping away the masks built on fear, doubt, and expectations. It's trading survival and silence for self-love, peeling back the layers of limitations that never belonged to you. This is your path to dream bigger than ever before—to become strong, whole, and free, and finally comfortable in your own skin. A journey of healing, embracing your worth, and building an abundant life on your own terms.

This is the foundation of everything I've learned, and it's one of the most profound lessons I want to share with you.

"Love is the most powerful force, but it cannot be forced."
– **Annamaria, The Red Heel BO$$**

Life is nothing without love, but we can't truly give or receive without shedding all the masks and bringing out our inner rebel. This book will help you do exactly that, so you can stop hiding, start living, and step into the life you've always known was meant for you.

For much of my life, I lived behind masks, obeying rules and fulfilling expectations, doing what I was told, and never considering my own needs. I thought love and attention were things I had to earn and deserve, not something I was inherently worthy of. Every rejection only made me try harder. I became consumed with people-pleasing, bending backward to accommodate others, hoping it would make me worthy of love and acceptance.

The side effects were devastating: indecisiveness, self-doubt, people-pleasing, and an endless need for validation. I never felt truly happy, but I didn't even realize it—I had never paused to consider my own preferences, desires, or dreams.

**In trying so hard to belong, I betrayed myself.
I lost myself behind the masks.**

I abandoned my own voice, truths, and dreams to fit into roles defined by others—society, culture, and family. I became a relational creature, molding myself into whatever version of "me" was needed to make others happy. I mastered the art of ensuring everyone else was okay, but at what cost? *I had no idea who I really was or what I truly wanted.*

Returning to You

There is a way back—a way to hear your own voice again. It begins with silencing the noise of expectations and reconnecting with the essence of who you are. It's about rediscovering what it means to *live authentically, without apology*, and embracing the truth that *happiness isn't something external*—money, expensive things, titles, or even relationships—*it's already within you.*

**Happiness comes from within, and from the relationship
you have with yourself. Give yourself unconditional love,
even more so when you don't receive it from others.**

Love, the real kind, starts with self-love.

When we learn to nurture that relationship, everything else begins to *align*. It's about realizing that *you are already enough, exactly as you are.* And when you live in alignment with that truth, you begin to operate on a higher frequency, becoming a magnet for the good things life has to offer.

The real essence is in finding harmony, *honoring who you are without compromise*, living authentically, and reclaiming your wholeness.

Let this be the reminder you need today:
Your voice matters.
Your needs are valid.
And your truest self is waiting to be heard.

Why This Book, and Why Now?

This book was born out of my own journey—a journey of losing myself, adapting to others' needs, and forgetting how to listen to my inner voice. But it's not just my story. Over the years, I've walked alongside other women—friends, clients, even strangers who became confidantes—each with their own battles, heartbreaks, and moments of rising, and I've recognized parts of my own story in theirs.

I know what it feels like to prioritize everyone else, to live by someone else's rules, and to wake up one day feeling completely disconnected from who you are. I also know the pain of believing that love and happiness are things you must earn—of living in a state of constant striving, thinking you have to prove your worth just to be accepted. Every time you're rejected, you try harder until the cycle leaves you empty.

But I also know what it feels like to break free—to reclaim your voice, honor your dreams, and rebuild a life rooted in abundance, authenticity, and self-love. And I've seen women around me do the same, each in their own courageous way.

I wrote this book because I want every woman who feels lost, unworthy, unseen, or unheard to know she is not alone. It's never too late to CLAIM your power, and to live a life that lights you up from the inside out. The rebel in you has always been there, she's just been hidden under masks you no longer need.

This is my WHY:

To help you reconnect with the person you *are* and flourish.

To remind you that your voice matters, your needs are valid, and your authentic self deserves to shine.

This book isn't just about rediscovering who you are—it's about stepping into your power as a woman. My mission is to help you achieve

emotional independence and financial freedom

because you are stronger, more capable, and more resilient than you realize. You can overcome anything life throws at you, and not just survive but thrive!

You can earn all the money you want. No explanations. No apologies.

Self-reliance should be a way of life, but too often, we've been conditioned to believe we can only achieve it with someone else. That's a lie society has told us for far too long. Healthy relationships naturally provide safety and security for both partners, but when life throws curveballs—injury, illness, loss—or relationships fall apart, we must be able to stand strong as individuals.

And when women do stand strong, something remarkable happens. We don't just survive—we create. Women are *natural leaders* and exceptional business owners, leading with their hearts, building connections, and creating impact. We are more than capable of making money while crafting beautiful and meaningful services—and the world needs more of it.

This is my personal WHY:

To lead by example for my daughters. I want them to see that they never have to bend into roles or expectations that don't align with who they are or feel uncomfortable with. They can define what a good life means to them, on their own terms.

Independence, empowerment, and freedom are not just ideals, but their birthright.

I'm constantly inspired by the younger generation of girls who are daring to question what's expected of them. Whether it's taking a gap year to discover the world beyond the classroom—boldly stepping away from the default path to choose one that honors their happiness—or using their voices to challenge injustices others are too afraid to name, these acts of rebellion, big or small, are powerful. One girl might write fierce opinion pieces about the unfair realities of underpaid careers, and another might speak up about the disturbing ethics behind animal testing at prestigious institutions. These aren't just moments of defiance, they're steps toward reclaiming joy, purpose, and personal truth.

As a mother, nothing makes me prouder than witnessing this kind of courage up close. Even if my girls prefer to stay out of my business world (fair enough!), their quiet strength, bold opinions, and refusal to settle remind me that the work we do—on ourselves and in the world—doesn't end with us. It echoes forward. And while their inner world is strong, the world they must navigate is still catching up—too often outdated, too often shaped by lingering notions of superiority. That's why the work ahead matters. I'll always wear my proud mom badge close to my heart, knowing every step we take makes the path a little clearer for them.

Built on Your Terms

So, where does this journey lead? What does true independence really look like?

It's *the freedom to build something that is entirely yours*—your business, your empire, your legacy. It's about creating a life where you don't just survive but thrive, fueled by your passion and purpose.

The journey begins with reclaiming your voice, rediscovering your power, and building the courage to own your truth.

And the catalyst that brings it all to life is how you *show up* in the world—your essence, your presence, the way you let others see the real you. Call it your personal brand if you like, but really, it's your unapologetic self in action.

Every moment in your life is a crossroads; you're either expressing your truth or wearing a mask someone else has chosen for you.

So the choice is yours: let the world project its filter onto you, or boldly show your true colors.

From there, the possibilities are limitless, because when you step fully into your potential, you create not just a business but a legacy.

This book is your guide to that journey—breaking free, stepping up, and stepping into the life you were always meant to lead. The first step is yours to take, and it starts right here.

The Story That Stopped Me in My Tracks

"I Left Him. I Was His Sex Slave and Housekeeper!"

It was a crisp morning, the kind where the sky feels endless, and possibilities seem within reach. I pulled into a petrol station, more focused on the long drive ahead than anything else. Just another stop, I thought. But life has a way of catching you off guard, reminding you of truths you didn't know you needed to see.

Inside the shop, the aroma of coffee greeted me, along with the familiar face of the barista. We'd met before. The first time, she had shared her dramatic weight loss story, hinting at a deeper narrative.

"Hello again," I said, smiling. "How are you?"

She smiled back, but her eyes were heavy. Then, as if a dam broke, she said words that stopped me in my tracks:

"I left him. I was his sex slave and housekeeper. Now my children are grown up, and I don't know what to do with myself. I was always a mom. What am I now?"

Her words were raw and jarring. At that moment, I didn't just see a barista or a stranger. I saw a woman who had spent her life in a cage she didn't even know existed until she stepped out of it. Now, she stood in the unfamiliar light of freedom, terrified and uncertain.

Her story is not what you'd hear every day, but it is not isolated. It reflected something universal—a truth about how society treats women.

Not all of us endure such blatant oppression, but many of us are placed in roles and labeled by expectations that diminish who we are.

We lose ourselves slowly—one compromise, one sacrifice, one silenced dream at a time. Until one day, we can't even name what we want anymore. Whether it's behind closed doors or in plain sight, this quiet erasure of identity is something so many women carry. Her words echoed in me because I knew that feeling too—not in the same way, but deeply enough to understand the grief of forgetting yourself.

The world tells us what we can't do, who we should be, and what we're worth. *And far too often, we believe it.*

Awakening Your Inner Rebel

A Daughter's Awakening

My own story isn't as stark, but it's no less significant. Growing up, I knew my father loved me. I carry so many fond memories of his kindness—the way his eyes softened when he called me by my nickname, the tenderness of his hand gently caressing my face, the safety I felt in his presence.

As a teenager, I faced my first real lesson in standing on my own feet. I had been studying jewelry making, and my father promised to open a shop for me. At first, it felt like a dream come true—my turn to pursue what I loved. But soon I realized the dream wasn't mine at all. The shop would belong to him, and I'd only be an employee.

It hurt. How could he love me yet not believe in my potential? That disappointment became a pivotal lesson in valuing myself and gaining my independence.

I didn't need anyone to create my own path to success.

My father didn't mean harm; his fears and traditions simply couldn't imagine a daughter owning her future. Rest in peace, Dad. I still feel your love. I miss you dearly.

His fears reflected a wider truth—how easily women are misunderstood, overlooked, and held back by collective, outdated beliefs. That's why I'm determined to help women awaken to their worth and power, to break free from those limitations and create the lives they deserve.

Healing From a Mother's Love

Growing up, I craved my mother's love more than anything. I cooked, cleaned, studied hard, followed the rules, avoided every teenage vice—no teenage antics, no drinking, no smoking, no disrespect—silently praying she'd notice and say, *"You did beautifully."* I did it all to prove how good I was, *how worthy I was of her love.*

One summer, I devoted myself entirely to caring for her. But when she refused to let me meet my friends at the park, the rebel in me snapped. I climbed out the window, crouched under the garden hedge, and scrambled through the fence. With the stealth of a secret agent, I darted between bushes, trying to evade the "search party." It was the most dramatic teenage jailbreak imaginable. For a moment, I felt free—yet the question lingered: Why was I never enough?

For years, those questions haunted me. Only later did I see that her silence wasn't about me. It was about her pain, her wounds, her survival.

Becoming a mother myself gave me a new perspective. I saw how much she must have carried, and I realized that her silence wasn't a reflection of my worth but of her own struggles. Despite the hurt, I never stopped longing for a connection with her.

Years later, a message from her nurse felt like the universe offering a second chance. When we spoke, the tension melted. She was warm, eager to share stories, and for the first time, I felt her love. That conversation marked the beginning of a new chapter for us—a relationship I never thought possible. We now talk regularly, sharing laughter, memories, and love.

Healing doesn't always have to erase the past. It can rewrite the present. My journey with my mother taught me that transformation is possible; *we* decide that the past will no longer dictate our future.

The Freedom of Letting Go

When you've shared years with someone, the end of that relationship can feel like stepping into a foreign land. A love that began in high school grew into a marriage that slowly fell out of balance—not through bad intentions, but through circumstance. I entered it with low confidence and self-esteem, pouring myself into who I thought I needed to be for him. Over time, marriage became a space where I shaped myself to fit someone else's world.

We slowly disconnected from the outer world, too, by spending nearly every moment together. There were good moments, and memories to cherish—our wedding, childbirth, adventures by lakes and rivers, holidays in new countries, bike rides, hikes, the thrill of new beginnings, and above all, our two incredible daughters. They were, and always will be, the greatest purpose of that relationship.

But as the years passed, the cracks deepened. Emotional strain and life's challenges became impossible to ignore. I've wrestled with these memories—some painful, some tender—I've come to see that this relationship was a chapter, not the entire story.

Letting go wasn't easy. There was anger, fear, and grief. Stepping into a new reality as a single parent felt like standing in a foreign land with no map. I had to navigate every challenge, every heartache, every moment of uncertainty for myself and for my girls—not just the glorious ones. Overnight, I became the solo mother, the hero who defeated giant spiders, the handyman assembling furniture, the plumber unclogging sinks.

The weight was heavy, both financially and emotionally—but with it came clarity: *I had the power to take charge of my life.*

I wasn't afraid anymore! I discovered a resilience I didn't know was there, quietly growing inside me all along.

Instead of dwelling on what I couldn't control, I focused on what I could. I embraced the role of provider, protector, and role model for my daughters. I showed them that strength isn't about having all the answers but about showing up, even when it's hard.

There's power in letting go—not to erase the past but to rewrite your future. This journey has been about reclaiming my independence, my confidence, and my voice. I'm no longer defined by the past, but by the steps I take every day to build a life of purpose, freedom, and love for myself and my girls. The mask is gone now, and the woman beneath it refuses to disappear again.

Personal Introduction

I am Annamaria, a proud mother of two incredible teen girls and the founder of The Red Heel BO$$, a business born from passion and purpose. My journey began in Hungary, where I was surrounded by a close-knit, loving family—grandparents, aunts, uncles, cousins, and friends—whose love and traditions grounded me with a deep *sense of connection and resilience.*

At 18, I underwent spinal surgery. Doctors warned me that I'd struggle with even basic activities, but I was determined to prove them wrong. Over the years, I not only regained strength but exceeded every expectation—two healthy pregnancies, two marathons, countless half-marathons. That experience taught me this: challenges aren't roadblocks; they're opportunities to grow and rise. That experience taught me a powerful lesson:

Challenges aren't roadblocks; they're opportunities to grow and rise.

Life took me across borders—first to England, then to New Zealand. Each move meant leaving behind family, culture, and certainty, but each one forced me to grow stronger, adapt faster, and widen my perspective. I've built lifelong friendships in the process.

Motherhood changed everything. My first daughter arrived, and my second three years later. With no extended family to lean on, I built a business during nap times and sleepless nights. Rest wasn't an option! What began as a small sewing venture grew into a thriving craft and festival business, connecting communities and teaching me to lead, negotiate, and innovate—all with my girls at the center.

Later, I returned to the workforce in New Zealand, climbing from entry-level to co-owner of a finance and business advisory firm within four years. But my entrepreneurial spirit was calling again. The Red Heel BO$$ began as a passion project to empower women toward emotional and financial freedom, and it has since grown into a multifaceted business—coaching, community, and a full-service branding and marketing agency.

Through all of it, my mission has stayed the same: to inspire, uplift, and equip women to build lives they love. Every chapter—from surgery to motherhood, migration to business—has taught me one truth:

resilience is a choice, and growth is always possible.

This book is not just my story; it's a guide to yours. We can overcome obstacles, embrace opportunities, and claim the lives we deserve.

The Red Heel BOSS

A Woman's Power to Transform

Women are creators, nurturers, and rebels. We take the raw materials of life—love, struggle, or hope—and transform them into something greater.

Yet too often this power is dismissed. For generations, society has told us we are too much—or not enough. Too emotional, too soft, too provocative. We've been boxed in, labeled, silenced, and told to shrink ourselves to fit the mold someone else created.

**This book is for every woman
who has ever doubted her worth.**

The mother juggling a million responsibilities, the professional second-guessing her voice in a room full of men, the woman staring in the mirror, wondering if she's enough. I see you.

This is a call to reclaim your power.

Your emotions are not a weakness—they are your superpower. They make you resilient, resourceful, and capable of navigating even the darkest storms. You don't have to dim your light to make others comfortable.

You are enough, exactly as you are.

We are not here to survive—we are here to thrive. It's time to rip off the masks, silence the doubters, and meet the version of you that's been waiting to run free. To awaken your inner rebel, step into your truth, and claim the life you deserve.

Let's go, Goddess. Your dreams are waiting.

Your 5 beautiful gifts!

Your life. Your dreams. Your terms.

Welcome to **The Red Heel BO$$ Community**
through reading this book.

Each Chapter of the NAKED! Womanizer will equip you with powers!

Turn what you read into real results with this exclusive *NAKED! Womanizer* gift bundle **valued at $399** packed with confidence rituals, boundary-setting tools, and self-love practices that actually stick.

They're **100% free for you** as a thank you for picking up this book.

Inside, you'll find high-impact tools and practices you can use immediately to step into your worth, confidence, and power:

- 👠 **5 Simple Steps to Find Balance** – 5 simple habits to balance work, life & relationships.
- 👠 **27 Ways to Overcome Negative Body Image** – cultivate real self-love.
- 👠 **Self-Intimacy Playbook** – quick daily practices for health, wealth & relationships.
- 👠 **Healthy Boundaries Cheat Sheet** – stop people-pleasing & start creating space with respect.
- 👠 **Feminine Affirmations for Success** – rewire your mind for abundance & achievement.

These are the exact practices, checklists, and rituals I've used and taught to create lasting transformation in myself and my clients.

👉 Grab your bundle here:
https://www.theredheelboss.com/womanizer5gifts/

Start living by your desires today.

Part 1: Awakening – Undone

"Like a wildflower breaking through the cracks, your strength has always been there, waiting for the right moment to bloom. Awakening is about rediscovering that strength—the unshakable force within you that refuses to stay buried, no matter how rocky the terrain. It's about embracing the beauty of imperfection, thriving in unexpected places, and realizing that you don't need permission to grow.

This is where the journey begins: a fearless burst of color in a world that underestimated your potential."

Chapter 1

The Ghost of Who I am

Every woman carries a quiet knowing, a truth buried under years of expectations, masks, and self-doubt.

Part 1 is about confronting the ghost of who you became for others, peeling back the layers of expectation, feeling the sting of what's been lost so you can rediscover the voice that's been yours: *you are more powerful than you've grown to believe.* This is the moment you choose yourself... and the first step toward the life that's been waiting for you.

When I was a little girl, I had a doctor's bag. Not just any doctor's bag—it was my most prized possession, filled with everything a little healer could need: a stethoscope, a thermometer, tiny bandages, and a plastic syringe. My dolls were my loyal patients, stoic and obedient, never once questioning my authority. I spent hours diagnosing their imaginary ailments, administering care, and marveling at my own ability to make them "better." In my world, I wasn't just a doctor. I was a magician, a miracle worker!

There was something about those moments that made me feel powerful, not in the sense of domination but of purpose. The kind of power that fills your chest with warmth and makes you believe you're capable of anything. I loved the way I could imagine a world where I mattered, where my hands brought comfort, and my ideas brought change. Even as a child, I had this deep, unshakable belief: *I could make things better.*

But, as all childhood stories go, mine didn't end with me standing in an operating room, scalpel in hand, ready to change the world. *Instead, the world changed me.*

The Good Girl Effect

It started small, as these things always do. One day, my parents were too busy to notice my latest "medical breakthrough", a Band-Aid masterpiece on my doll's plastic arm. Another day, a teacher's raised eyebrow told me that my dream of being a doctor wasn't quite realistic for someone like me. "You're so caring," they'd say. "You'll make a wonderful wife and mother someday." The implication hung heavy: that was the height of my ambition.

And so, little by little, the bold, imaginative girl with her doctor's bag began to fade. Not because she wanted to, but because *she learned it was easier to shrink than to fight.* To *blend into the background rather than to stand out.* To *ghost herself rather than risk being ghosted by others.*

By the time I reached my teenage years, I was a master at disappearing. I said the right things, wore the right clothes, and followed the unspoken rules.

I became the "good girl", not too loud, not too ambitious, not too much.

My dreams of healing turned into vague hopes of "making a difference" someday, though I wasn't sure how. The doctor's bag collected dust in the corner of my room, a relic of a life I no longer recognized.

The Societal Blueprint

Society handed me a blueprint for my life, and it was painfully simple: Be a wife. Be a mother. Be good. It didn't matter that I had other dreams. Dreams were frivolous, a luxury for someone else—someone with fewer responsibilities, fewer expectations.

My job was to follow the script,
not to write my own story.

And so, I did. I checked the boxes, played the roles, and told myself it was ok. But deep down, I felt like a ghost. The girl who once believed she could do anything was now haunting the edges of her own life, too afraid to step into the light.

When the Light Flickered

Every now and then, there were moments when the light flickered — a brief reminder of who I used to be. Like the time I helped a friend through a crisis and felt that old, familiar warmth in my chest. Or the time I stood up for myself at work and felt the rush of being heard. These moments were rare, but *they were enough to remind me that the ghost inside me wasn't gone.* She was just waiting, patiently, for me to remember her.

One night, as I sat in the quiet of my home, I found myself holding my daughter's toy stethoscope. It wasn't mine, but it felt familiar. The plastic felt cheap, and the tubing was bent, but as I held it, a memory flooded back, *a memory of a little girl who believed she could heal the world.*

And for the first time in years, *I let myself wonder:* What happened to her?

The First Step Back

Recognizing the ghost of who you were is a painful process. It forces you to *confront the ways you've abandoned yourself, the dreams you've buried, and the person you've left behind.* But it's also a chance to **reclaim her**. To take that first, brave step toward becoming whole again.

I didn't wake up the next morning with my life magically transformed. There was no grand epiphany, no cinematic montage of triumph. But there was a decision: to stop shrinking, stop hiding, stop ghosting myself. *To believe, once again, that I could make things better, starting with my own life.*

Takeaway: Reclaiming Your Powers

You've spent years adapting, shrinking, and disappearing. But the person you were—the dreamer, the doer, the believer—is still there, waiting for you to notice her.

Take a moment to reflect on your own ghost.
Who were you before the world told you who to be?
What dreams did you have before you learned to doubt them?
And what would it take to begin reclaiming her?

This is just the first step of the journey, but it's the most important one. *Because before you can awaken the powerful woman within, you must first acknowledge the ghost of who you were.*

Pause & Reflect

Write a letter to your younger self. Tell her what you remember about her dreams and what you wish she knew about the woman she's becoming.

End with a promise to honor her voice moving forward.

Chapter 2

The Masks We Wear

When I was little, my dolls never questioned me. They never doubted my diagnoses or laughed at my solutions. My doctor's bag and I were the ultimate authority in my imaginary hospital, and I never had to worry about what anyone thought. But somewhere along the way, that changed. I started to care—too much—about how others perceived me.

As I grew older, I learned an unspoken rule: What people say about you when you're not around holds more weight than what they say to your face. It's as though the world splits into two stages: the one where we perform and the one where we're discussed. And who wants to be the subject of whispers? The idea of people talking behind my back, dissecting my flaws, or mocking my choices became unbearable. I thought if I could just be the "right" version of myself, I could escape their judgment. So, I started wearing masks.

The Masks Begin

The first mask I wore was simple: the "good girl." The one who always said "please" and "thank you," followed the rules, and never made a scene. This mask made people happy, and I liked making people happy. It felt good to be liked. But over time, this mask became less about who I was and more about who I thought others wanted me to be.

As I got older, the masks multiplied. There was the "perfect student" who never let anyone see her struggle, the "devoted partner" who sacrificed her own needs for someone else's happiness, and the "model employee" who worked late into the night to prove she was worth her paycheck. Each mask was carefully crafted, polished, and worn with pride. But each one also came with a cost.

The masks were heavy. They muffled my voice and blurred my identity. The little girl who used to feel powerful and confident with her doctor's bag was now terrified of standing out. Instead of using her voice, she let it grow quiet, hiding behind roles and personas that felt safer than being her true self.

The Doctor's Ghost Returns

That fear followed me into adulthood, into the conference rooms and meeting tables where I sat silently, afraid to speak up. I'd have an idea—a good one—but I'd second-guess myself.

I'd rehearse responses in my head, mentally edit them three times, then say nothing at all. The fear of being wrong—or worse, being dismissed—kept my mouth shut. I wasn't just afraid of speaking; I was afraid of *not being taken seriously*.

What if it's a stupid idea? What if they laugh? What if they think I don't belong here?

Every time, the ghost of my childhood doctor's bag would prompt me, *You're supposed to make things better. But how can you do that if you don't speak up?*

It was like a script etched into my nervous system—be helpful, not disruptive. Don't challenge. Don't question. Just nod, agree, and blend in. I thought that was how you earned respect, when really, it was how I disappeared.

Still, the mask of the "agreeable team player" stayed firmly in place. I convinced myself that silence was safer.

Then one day, I couldn't stay silent. I don't remember what triggered it—maybe frustration, maybe a tiny spark of courage—but I finally spoke up. I shared an idea that had been circling in my mind for weeks. My voice felt shaky and too loud, like an out-of-tune instrument in a silent room. For a moment, the room went still, and I braced for the worst. But then someone said, "That's not a bad idea." Another person added, "I hadn't thought of that. It's worth investigating."

The recognition felt foreign, almost uncomfortable. But it also felt good, like stepping into sunlight after hiding in the shadows for too long. I realized that my fear of judgment had been holding me back more than any actual judgment ever could. The masks I wore weren't protecting me—they were suffocating me.

Unmasking Myself

Once I saw the cracks in the masks, I couldn't unsee them. *I began to notice how often I performed for others instead of being true to myself.* I'd laugh at jokes I didn't find funny, agree to tasks I didn't want to do, and downplay my ideas so I wouldn't seem too bold or ambitious. Every time I did, I felt that little girl with her doctor's bag fade further away.

Unmasking myself wasn't easy. It's not like you can just rip the masks off and suddenly feel free. They've been part of me for so long that taking them off feels like losing a piece of myself. But piece by piece, I started peeling them away. I stopped saying "yes" when I used to agree. I started sharing my thoughts, even when they felt messy or imperfect.

And I let myself be seen—not the polished version, but the real one.

The Cost of Masks

Wearing masks might keep you safe from judgment, but it also keeps you away from connection. When you hide behind roles and personas, you rob yourself of the chance to be truly known—and truly loved—for who you are. The people who matter don't want the mask. They want you.

The girl with the doctor's bag didn't care what anyone thought. She cared about making things better. She cared about healing. And the moment I started taking off my masks, I began to remember her. Not as someone I used to be, but as someone I could still become.

Takeaway: Peeling Back the Layers

The masks you wear might feel like armor, but they're really cages. It's time to start peeling them back and uncovering your true self. Start small. Ask yourself:

What roles am I playing in my life?
Which roles feel authentic, and which feel like masks?
What would happen if I let people see the real me?

The journey of unmasking is uncomfortable, but it's also liberating. Because beneath the masks is the person you've always been—the one who's been waiting to be seen.

Pause & Reflect

Journal about the roles you play.

Write down the masks you wear and the reasons you wear them.

Then, choose one mask to take off this week. Maybe it's saying "no" to something you don't want to do. Maybe it's sharing an idea at work. Maybe it's telling someone how you really feel.

Start small, but start.

Chapter 3

The Roles We Play

In many households, especially in traditional settings, boys carry the legacy. Girls? We're often expected to carry the grace, the silence, the invisible load of being *good*. That's just how society has worked for generations — quietly assigning value based on gender.

Growing up, I witnessed this play out in real time. The spotlight naturally fell on the son, with cars, property, the family business, and financial backing all flowing his way. It wasn't just favoritism; it was systemic. As a daughter, my role was clear: smile, study, and stay in line.

Was it because I was the second child or because I was a girl?

I have zero intentions to blame anyone. My family gave me so much: a safe home, delicious food, family vacations, and an excellent education. I'm deeply grateful for all of it.

But gratitude and grief can exist side by side.

Because the truth is — I never truly felt seen or significant.

In my early twenties, I was given something that, on the surface, looked like independence. And I was truly grateful — it was a gesture of care and support that not everyone is fortunate enough to receive.

But in my family, for some, opportunities came with full ownership and freedom; for others, they came "protected," with invisible strings still attached. I understood the reasoning, but the unspoken message was clear: my independence would always exist within boundaries.

The gift itself was gratefully treasured, yet it carried the shadow of a quiet truth about the roles we were expected to play.

They believed they were doing the right thing. And maybe, by old standards, they were. But what good is protection when it reinforces the feeling that you're not trusted—not *truly* seen?

What I do know is that love in my family showed up in many forms. My grandparents—on both sides—saw all of us grandchildren as equals, and from what I could tell, their own children too. They looked after us with a deep, unwavering care that made each of us feel special.

As a child, that love from my grandparents—and from my aunties—was a source of pure comfort. I treasure the memories of being in the kitchen with them, helping in their gardens, going on holidays, and celebrating Easter, Christmas, and family gatherings. Even the quiet, one-on-one moments still fill me with warmth and joy when I think back.

Those precious times reminded me that I was deeply loved—and that love, in all its different expressions, would be a part of me forever.

The Good Girl Script

I tried to play the part they wanted me to play. The good girl. The responsible one. I studied hard, stayed away from alcohol and drugs, and avoided recklessness. I followed the rules. And yet, it was never enough.

Being "good" was supposed to guarantee love, approval, or at least peace. But somewhere along the line, I started to realize that goodness — in the way it was defined for girls like me — came with no reward. Just more silence, more pressure, more ways to fall short. It wasn't about who I was; it was about how well I could perform a version of myself that fit their expectations.

No matter how much I bent myself into the shape they required, there was always a hint of dissatisfaction, a shadow of disappointment.

"Why can't she be more like...?"

My name was spoken in complaints, often to the wider family, where I became a source of gossip rather than pride. My dreams were dismissed before they even had the chance to spread their wings. I felt insignificant. A nobody. Belittled. Nonexistent.

And worse, I felt guilty for not being the daughter I was supposed to be, even though I didn't know how else to try.

I didn't know how to breathe, let alone thrive.

A Silent Sadness

The weight of expectations had a way of shaping everything—from how I viewed myself to how I showed up in the world. I wasn't just trying to meet the bar set by others; I was trying to justify my very existence.

I became a master of self-surveillance, constantly scanning my behavior, tone, and even facial expressions. Would this be acceptable? Did I say too much? Not enough? I measured my worth through the lens of what others might think—long before they even said a word. Living became a performance, and I forgot what it felt like to simply *be*.

That heaviness crept into my adulthood, not as outright defiance, but as a quiet compliance.

It wasn't the loud kind of pain. It was the kind that sits with you at dinner. The kind that folds laundry with you. It slips into your daily routines until you forget it's there—until one day, you don't recognize the person in the mirror, because she's been edited down to please everyone else.

At work, I held back my thoughts and ideas, unsure if my voice mattered or if I'd be taken seriously. At home, I bent to the needs of others, believing it was my duty to serve rather than be heard. Taking a break with a book or a cuppa was unimaginable. Taking a full hour for a workout? Outrageous. I secretly envied my friends who got away for girls' weekends. How was that possible? A full weekend of fun without constant chores?

The impact of living under that weight wasn't immediate; it was cumulative. Like a slow erosion of self-belief, the weight became normal, even though it was anything but.

That moment didn't erase years of self-doubt, but cracked something open.

It reminded me that the weight of others' expectations was never mine to bear.

So I knew I needed to begin working on my self-esteem and self-worth.

The Awakening

It wasn't until my forties that I truly began to feel the weight of all the bending and conforming I'd done. I started to see how much of myself I'd sacrificed to fit into a mold that wasn't mine and shouldn't have existed in the first place.

I had checked all the boxes, played all the roles — the dutiful daughter, the supportive partner, the high-achieving woman — but underneath it all, there was a quiet ache. An emptiness I couldn't name. I was successful on the outside, but on the inside, I was lost in layers of identities built to please everyone but myself.

The realization came slowly, but painfully: My childhood wounds—the constant feeling of being invisible and insignificant—had left cracks in the foundation of my entire life. Those cracks had spread into my relationship, my work, my business, and even what I treasure the most: motherhood. I'd been so busy trying to meet the expectations self-imposed or placed on me that I never stopped to ask:

How do I want to turn up for myself?

The version of me no longer existed. I was evolving, growing, healing—and it came with *letting go* of ideas, things, and people in my life. It wasn't about blame; it was about boundaries. For the first time, I was beginning to define what happiness means to me, and

I realized it wasn't about keeping everyone else comfortable *at the expense of my own.*

In my relationships, I started to honor myself. I no longer tolerated being dismissed or overlooked. I drew boundaries that protected my energy and created space for new things. It wasn't easy, and it wasn't without pain, but it was inevitable. For the first time, I wasn't just surviving—I was living.

In meetings, I began to advocate for my thoughts and contributions, no longer keeping them to myself. It was like an out-of-body experience at first, but each time, I grew a little stronger. Every acknowledgment—every "that's not a bad idea" or "I hadn't thought of that"—became a crack in the armor of self-doubt I'd worn for so long.

In my business, I stopped pretending. For 18 months, I'd clung to the idea of being an entrepreneur, but the truth was, I didn't believe in myself. I was stuck in the creation mode, but never promoted anything. I was too afraid to step out and show the world what I could truly offer. But as I worked on myself, something shifted. I began creating a personal brand that truly reflected who I was and what I stood for. I let my mission and values shine through, attracting the right tribe and finally feeling aligned with my purpose.

This awakening wasn't about any one moment. It was the culmination of doing the work—unpacking my childhood trauma, redefining what success and happiness looked like for me, and finding the courage to let my voice be heard. It was about realizing that I deserved to take up space in my work, my business, my relationships, and my own life.

That awakening was an adjustment. It hurt to realize how much of me I'd lost by trying to meet everyone else's expectations.

I grieved the version of me that knew how to be perfect by constantly trying to earn love, prove her worth, and be accepted. In that grief, I let myself cry, crumble, and sit with the silence I used to fill by getting busy with chores.

Letting her go wasn't easy—she had protected me for years. But she was built on survival, not self-love. And to grow, I had to release her.

In doing so, I set myself free.

And somewhere beneath the pain, I found a quiet power. A new kind of peace. One rooted far from people-pleasing or proving, but in presence. I was no longer chasing validation—I was coming home to myself.

For the first time, I began to ask myself: *What do I want? What do I need? What would it look like to live for me, instead of for everyone else?*

The Universal Burden

This is also the story of so many women, not just mine.

We've been raised on a silent curriculum—one that teaches us to shrink, to serve, to smile even when it hurts. The messaging may be subtle, but it's powerful: Be agreeable. Be nurturing. Don't take up too much space. And if you dare to dream bigger, make sure it doesn't inconvenience anyone else.

We wear a thousand hats, balancing the expectations of family, work, and society. We're supposed to be everything to everyone: the perfect mother, the devoted partner, the high-performing employee, the selfless friend... and don't forget to mention being a Sex-Goddess. We're supposed to do it all effortlessly, without complaint.

For stay-at-home moms, the guilt is different but just as heavy. Society might say their work isn't "real" because it doesn't come with a paycheck. But raising the next generation—the future leaders, thinkers, and decision-makers of the world—is one of the most important contributions anyone can make.

Creating a safe space for children to express themselves, grow confidently, and learn to think outside the box is the most valuable work and contribution one can make.

Yet we're conditioned to feel like we're never enough. We sacrifice ourselves to make sure everyone else is okay, but we rarely ask if *we* are okay. It's a conflict we feel deeply when life starts to slip out of balance and alignment.

That's when the quiet resentment creeps in. Not because we don't love our people or our work, but because we've disappeared somewhere along the way. We start to realize that meeting everyone else's needs has come at the cost of abandoning our own. And it's in that realization that something begins to stir—a faded voice that says: *You matter too.*

We want to be everything for others, *but we also need space to be everything for ourselves.*

The Backpack We Carry

If I had to describe the weight of expectations, I'd call it a backpack. It starts light, something you barely notice, but over time, people keep adding to it. A rock for being a good girl. A rock for being the perfect mother. A rock for saying yes when you wanted to say no. Before you know it, the backpack is so heavy that you can barely keep moving forward.

But here's the secret: That backpack isn't locked. You can take it off. Not all at once, but piece by piece. Start by letting go of the rocks that don't serve you. It's not easy, and it's not instant. But it is possible.

Takeaway: Lightening the Load

The weight of expectations isn't yours to carry forever. It's time to start asking: *Whose expectations are these? Do they serve me? Do I want to keep carrying them?*

They might feel overwhelming, but you don't have to carry it alone. And you don't have to carry it forever.

Our community of amazing women provides support, uplifts each other, celebrates one another, and we cry, laugh, and have fun in the Feminine Energy and Business Mastery community. This is the beginning of lightening your load, one step at a time.

Pause & Reflect

Take a moment to reflect on the rocks in your backpack.

Write down the expectations you've been carrying, whether they come from family, society, or yourself.

Choose one expectation to let go of this week. Maybe it's the idea that you have to say yes to every request. Maybe it's the guilt for not being the "perfect" parent or partner.

Whatever it is, take one rock out of the backpack and set it down.

Chapter 4

It Hurts Like Hell

No matter how much we achieve or how well we do, we struggle to see our value. We run our lives on autopilot, not even recognizing what's wrong. We've simply learned to live with it. These coping mechanisms become symptoms of a deeper root issue that keeps us stuck, drained, and defeated.

Negative Nancy, that mean girl in your head, steps in with a running commentary of self-doubt and fear. The truth is, these emotions are exhausting. They rob us of joy and confidence, making it harder to thrive.

We internalize so many messages—about how we should look, act, love, lead, mother, and succeed. Over time, these messages become a part of our inner dialogue. We stop questioning them and start believing them. That voice in our head? It's not even ours. It's a messy collage of societal noise, childhood conditioning, and fear dressed up as logic. No wonder we feel like we're constantly falling short.

Let's break down what we're experiencing and how it manifests, and challenge whether these beliefs are even true, with a dash of humor, because, honestly, Negative Nancy deserves a little roasting.

The Things That Universally Connect Women

The things that universally connect women aren't always the warm, fuzzy ones we put on Pinterest boards. They're the shared struggles we don't post online—the ones that live quietly in our minds but feel heavy in our hearts.

They're the doubts we carry into the boardroom, the guilt we pack in our handbags, and the fears that show up uninvited just when we think we've got it all together.

We may come from different cultures, countries, and backgrounds, but if you gather a group of women in one room, chances are, you'll hear echoes of the same inner battles. And while that's heartbreaking in some ways, it's also strangely comforting—because it means you're not crazy, you're not broken, and you're definitely not alone.

So, let's name them. Let's drag them out from the shadows, shine a light on them, and maybe laugh a little in their face. Because once you see them clearly, they start to lose their grip.

Imposter Syndrome

→ **What We Go Through:** It's the voice that whispers, "Who do you think you are?" You feel like a fraud, convinced your success is a fluke and you'll be exposed at any moment. It's like you're waiting for someone to burst in and yell, "Gotcha! Give back that promotion—we know you're faking it!"

→ **Common Thoughts:** "I don't belong here." "Everyone else is smarter." "I've just been lucky."

→ **Challenge It:** Is there actual evidence that you're a fraud, or is this just Negative Nancy getting creative? *Why would I simply believe what she is saying?*

Self-Doubt

→ **What We Go Through:** You second-guess every decision, questioning whether you're capable or deserving. It's like walking with a pebble in your shoe—small, annoying, and somehow making every step miserable.

→ **Common Thoughts:** "What if I'm wrong?" "I'm not good enough." "I'm so stupid, I never get anything right."

→ **Challenge It:** Would someone who isn't capable even care this much about getting it right? Could you trust your instincts instead of assuming failure, or at least take off the shoe and check for the pebble?

Fear

→ **What We Go Through:** Fear shows up as fear of failure, judgment, or even success. It's the emotion that whispers, "Better stay quiet; it's safer here in your little cocoon of mediocrity."

→ **Common Thoughts:** "What if I mess up?" "What if they don't like me?" "What if they think I'm a joke?"

→ **Challenge It:** What's the worst that could happen if you tried? Would it really be worse than spending another year listening to Fear's Greatest Hits?

Guilt

→ **What We Go Through:** Guilt makes you feel like no matter what you do, it's never enough. It's like carrying a backpack full of rocks labeled "Not a good enough mom," "Terrible friend," and "Selfish for wanting time alone."

→ **Common Thoughts:** "I should be doing more." "I'm failing as a mother/partner/professional." "I'm so selfish for wanting this."

→ **Challenge It:** Would you expect someone else to meet these impossible standards? What if guilt is just the rock you're meant to put down?

Shame

→ **What We Go Through:** Shame tells you that you're not just failing; you're fundamentally flawed. It's like wearing a name tag that says, "Hi, I'm a Mess."

→ **Common Thoughts:** "I'm such a failure." "Everyone can see I'm a mess." "Why can't I get it together?"

→ **Challenge It:** Is shame really helping you grow, or is it just keeping you stuck? Could you show yourself the same compassion you'd offer a friend—or at least take off the name tag?

Perfectionism

→ **What We Go Through:** Perfectionism demands more than you can give, convincing you that anything less than flawless is failure. It's like having a drill sergeant in your head yelling, "Do better! Do it perfectly! Or don't do it at all!"

→ **Common Thoughts:** "I can't make mistakes." "If it's not perfect, it's worthless." "I'm only valuable when I succeed."

→ **Challenge It:** Can you redefine success as progress instead of perfection? Or at least tell your inner drill sergeant to take a lunch break?

Anxiety

→ **What We Go Through:** Anxiety is the constant hum of worry that something will go wrong. It's like having a hyperactive smoke alarm in your head, going off for no reason.

→ **Common Thoughts:** "What if I made the wrong choice?" "I'll never get everything done." "Everyone's judging me."

→ **Challenge It:** Are these fears based on reality or just worst-case scenarios? What's the kindest thing you could say to yourself at this moment?

Negative Self-Talk

→ **What We Go Through:** Negative self-talk is relentless, amplifying your flaws and dismissing your strengths. It's like letting a mean girl live in your head rent-free.

→ **Common Thoughts:** "I'm so stupid." "I can't do anything right." "I'll never be good enough."

→ **Challenge It:** Would you let someone speak to your best friend that way? Why let Negative Nancy get away with it?

Takeaway: Taking Back Your Power

These emotions aren't who you are; they're symptoms of a deeper issue, coping mechanisms that have overstayed their welcome. They've dulled your spark, kept you stuck, and made you doubt yourself. *But they don't have to define you.*

How can you stop letting Negative Nancy and her crew control your life, emotions, and decisions?

Maybe it's time to evict her and remind her she's not on the lease.

The first step is to recognize them for what they are.

The next is to refuse to give them power.

Because the truth is, *you deserve better*. You deserve to live fully, unapologetically, and free from the weight of these lies. And if Nancy has something to say, you can tell her to take a seat in the farthest corner of the room.

Chapter 5

The Turning Point

The moment of transformation rarely comes wrapped in certainty or ease. For me, it began the day I became a mother. There's something about holding a new life in your hands that starts reshaping everything you thought you knew about yourself. But the real turning point—the moment I **chose** transformation—was when I decided to stand up for my daughters.

It wasn't a grand, dramatic declaration. It was quiet, filled with fear, and laced with doubt. I knew that expressing myself and challenging the status quo would come with consequences. After all, I'd lived that story before: Speak up, and you get told off. It's the pattern I'd grown up with—one I thought I'd left behind but found myself reliving. But this time, it was different. This time, I wasn't standing up just for myself. I was standing up for them, for love, and that overrode every fear.

Facing Fear, Step by Step

There's a misconception that bravery means you're fearless. I'm here to tell you it doesn't work that way. I can speak for myself when I say I was terrified. My inner voice, shaky as it was, kept telling me, "*You have to do this.*" Each step felt ginormous, like climbing a mountain barefoot in the rain and mud.

Fear didn't disappear; it just stopped being the driver. I learned to move with it, to breathe through it. I still shook, but I shook forward. And that alone was progress.

I remember clearly the knot in my stomach, the rasp in my voice, the lump in my throat, the tightness in my chest. My body spoke the fear I tried so hard to suppress. But I showed up anyway. Quivering, but present. Doubtful, but determined.

With every act of speaking up or refusing to sacrifice, no matter how small, I felt my power growing. It wasn't overnight. It wasn't glamorous. It looked like asking for help and support, making phone calls I dreaded, saying "no" when I usually said "yes," and starting to set and communicate boundaries, or letting go of people who didn't respect them. These were the quiet revolutions that slowly stitched my self-trust back together.

I didn't wake up one day fully confident and ready to conquer the world. My confidence came piece by piece, step by step, through the tears and uncertainty.

Standing by my girls meant facing not only external battles but also internal ones. Self-doubt was a constant companion, asking, "*Who are you to think you can do this?*" But I reminded myself: *Who am I not to? If I don't lead with courage, how will they learn to?* I was breaking generational patterns and building a brighter future (So I hope!).

With each decision to push forward, I began to feel something new—a quiet pride, not the loud, boastful kind.

It was the kind of pride that grows in your chest when you know, deep down, you're doing the right thing, even if it terrifies you.

Liberation in the Little Things

The changes didn't happen overnight. It was a rollercoaster of emotions—ups and downs, tears and joy, setbacks and breakthroughs. But as I persisted, I began to notice little moments of liberation. The peace at home after a hard-fought boundary. The sound of my daughters' laughter filling the house. The sight of them becoming confident, happy, and whole.

Slowly, I began to trust myself, to feel proud of the woman and mother I was becoming.

And then there was the shift within myself.

I started to feel free—not completely, not all at once, but in little pockets of my life.

I found relief in shaping my own days, making decisions for my family, and attracting beautiful people and opportunities into my life. With self-improvement came an unexpected blessing: massive support from new friendships. The usual "How do you do's" on social media transformed into fast-tracked connections and unbreakable bonds. These friends became my anchors, offering a shoulder to cry on, reminding me how far I'd come in such a short amount of time, and celebrating me as a person, a friend, a mother, and a CEO. They lifted my mood with jokes, created experiences that nourished my soul, and stood by me every step of the way. It was a kind of support I never knew I could have, but am forever grateful for.

The Universal Need for Change

Every woman has her turning point, and it doesn't come when everything is fine.

It's that moment when the pain of staying the same becomes greater than the fear of change.

Maybe it's when you've given so much of yourself to others that there's nothing left for you. Maybe it's when you realize the life you're living no longer fits who you are or who you want to be. Or maybe it's just a quiet, persistent voice that says, *"Enough."*

We've all been there. Afraid of making the leap but even more afraid of staying stuck. Because deep down, we know the truth:

Growth is uncomfortable. It's messy. It's painful. But it's also inevitable.

It's like ripping off a band-aid. The sting is temporary, but the healing that follows is worth everything.

The Quiet Voice of Courage

What I learned through this journey is that confidence doesn't have to be loud and shout from the rooftops to make powerful changes. Sometimes, the most profound transformations come from the quietest voices—the ones that speak in whispers but carry the weight of your entire heart.

Being brave doesn't mean you're not afraid. It means you feel the fear, acknowledge it, and move forward anyway, guided by the deep knowing that *change is necessary and transformation is coming*. It means trusting that the little voice inside you, however faint, is leading you toward a better version of yourself.

Takeaway: The First Step

Turning points aren't about knowing the whole path ahead; they're about taking the first step, however small it may be. It's about **choosing yourself, your loved ones, and the life you want over the fear that's been holding you back.** And here's the secret:

Every step you take makes the next one a little easier, until one day, you look back and realize you're no longer climbing—you're soaring.

To move forward with clarity and confidence, we need to learn to recognize the different voices influencing our state of being:

The Inner Voices:

→ **The Loud Voice (Ego):** Ego has a talent for turning the volume up on bad advice. It convinces you that you're the star of the show—whether that's overestimating your abilities or making you show off (hello, overlifting in the gym or running too long!). It says, *"Go on, they'll think you're amazing!"* making you do things you wouldn't otherwise. Ego is the background actor pushing you to win, not the hero it pretends to be.

→ **The Doubtful Voice:** It's usually the one giving bad advice, shouting fear, doubt, or comparison, and thrives on keeping you small, constantly criticizing you. It says things like, *"What if you're wrong?"* or *"You can never make it happen."* It feeds on your insecurities and can feel relentless. But remember, this voice thrives on your attention—and you have the power to redirect it.

→ **The Quiet Voice (Inner Guide):** The inner guide is like that friend who doesn't shout over the music but always knows the right thing to say. It's steady, calm, and wise, nudging you toward the choices that align with your deepest values. Unlike ego, it doesn't demand attention—it offers guidance, patiently waiting for you to tune in. When you listen, you'll find it's the compass that always points you in the right direction.

The Outside Voices:

→ **Judgments:** Not every opinion or piece of advice deserves your attention. Some outside voices are like that annoying song stuck in your head—persistent but not helpful. Setting boundaries lets you tune out the noise and focus on what truly matters.

→ **The Guardians:** Then there are the voices that uplift. Believing in your higher powers—whether it's the universe, God, or whatever resonates with you—offers a sense of guidance beyond your limits. Trusting this guidance means letting go of old constraints and stepping into possibilities you never thought possible.

The answers you need are already within you.

You have the wisdom, intuition, experience, and heart to guide you.

Remember: before every great turning point, **there is a season of being undone**. That's not weakness—it's the breaking open that makes space for your strength to rise.

Your Companion for Change

Pause here. You deserve a moment (or as many as you need) to breathe.

Give yourself the gift of slowing down, reflecting, and truly embracing what you've just read.

Loved this part of the book?

Take it to the next level with your **companion workbook**
designed as your personal journal
to help you apply these lessons in your own life.

You're creating new habits, and you deserve all the support along the way.

Inside, you'll find thoughtful prompts, practical exercises, and dedicated space to explore your next steps — so these shifts don't just inspire you, they become part of your daily reality.

Download it here:
https://www.theredheelboss.com/womanizerworkbook

(or simply scan the QR Code in the image above)

Part 2: The Shift – Unafraid

"Like a sunflower unapologetically turning its face toward the sun, this is your time to rise with boldness, strength, and a willingness to rewrite your story. The Shift isn't just about growth—it's about stepping into the light, unafraid of the shadows you leave behind."

Chapter 1

Rewriting the Narrative

We've discovered the masks holding us back in Part 1.

You've done the groundwork, faced the truth, named the patterns, and let go of the versions of yourself that no longer serve you after awakening from the harsh truths of a dissatisfying life.

Now, Part 2 is where the energy shifts.

This is your time to rise with boldness, strength, and a willingness to rewrite your story. The Shift is about growth as much as about stepping into the light, unafraid of the shadows you leave behind.

In the next chapters, we're going to challenge the myths you've believed, call back your power, and rebuild your life on your terms. We'll talk about happiness that isn't tied to anyone else, self-love that isn't conditional, boundaries that protect your glow, and confidence so unshakable it becomes magnetic.

Your Story, Your Rules – Breaking Free from Old Scripts

It's hard to face it—our inner critic is the meanest girl we've ever met, and she's been running the show for way too long, hogging the mic and calling the shots. She insists you stay in your comfort zone because 'What if you fail?' and 'Who do you think you are?'

It's time to fire her! She is NOT YOU. She is a hand-me-down from years of conditioning, and it's time to swap her out for the one that cheers you on.

What Are Limiting Beliefs, Really?

Limiting beliefs aren't just random fears; they're sneaky little lies we collect like dodgy souvenirs along the way. They sound like:

→ *"It's too late to start over."*
→ *"You're not smart enough for that."*
→ *"Good things don't happen to people like you."*

They don't show up waving red flags; they tiptoe in wearing the perfect disguise: "common sense" or "being realistic." And because most of them were handed to us when we were too young to tell the truth from total BS and complete nonsense, we just let them unpack their bags and move in.

Over time, they settle in and start decorating the walls of our minds, as if they own the place.

As kids, we're bold and fearless—we climb trees, use our imagination to make up stories, and believe anything is possible. But as we grow, the "rules" pile up:

→ *"You can't say that."*
→ *"What will people think?"*
→ *"It's too dangerous. Don't do that, you'll hurt yourself!"*

Suddenly, that adventurous spirit fades, and we're stuck making decisions based on fear rather than curiosity.

For me, food was one of those beliefs. Food is emotional—deeply tied to memories and rituals. I remember the childhood joy of Sunday afternoons, sitting at a sunlit kitchen table with the smell of roast chicken wafting through the house. Food was comfort, celebration, and family.

So when I began questioning what I'd always believed about food—how it affects us, how it's produced—it felt like I was betraying a part of myself.

But then, I couldn't unsee what I'd learned. And once you see a truth that deep, you can't go back to pretending.

Breaking My Own Script: Beyond Food

It started when my late friend, diagnosed with stage 4 cancer, began exploring food as a way to support her body during treatment. Her teachings on the effects of food and what her body could tolerate opened a door for me I didn't even know existed. Through her, I learned how much our choices impact our bodies and minds.

Rethinking everything I'd been taught about food and health. I went all in, researching late into the night. I watched video after video, each one more gut-wrenching than the last. I saw mother cows separated from their calves, their cries echoing in the air as their babies were taken away. I learned about the treatment of animals on factory farms and how the food we consume is linked to so much unnecessary suffering—not just theirs, but ours too.

Every new discovery felt like a betrayal of the comforting childhood meals I'd loved. But I couldn't turn away. I saw how my own choices were connected to a system built on pain, and

I realized I couldn't keep living by the rules someone else had handed me.

Letting go wasn't easy. Food is tied to culture, family, and identity. But rewriting this part of my narrative was *the most freeing thing* I've ever done. It was *beyond* food. *It was* about *taking back control of my story* and *honoring my late friend. I chose to honor her* not only in her food choices but also by embracing happiness, rather than grieving the life she could no longer share with her 2 young children and beloved husband.

The Stories We Inherit

When you're a child—two, three, four years old—you don't have the frame of reference to question the moments that shape you. You simply absorb them. The way people look at you, speak to you, or include you—or don't—becomes part of the story you believe about yourself. Without realizing it, you internalize messages about your worth, your place in the world, and what you're "allowed" to ask for.

I've worked with so many women whose early experiences planted these invisible seeds. One beautiful client grew up in a loving home, yet certain extended relatives subtly kept her at arm's length. There were no harsh words, no outright rejection—just an unspoken disapproval that lingered like a shadow. Over time, that shadow grew into the belief: *"I'm not enough."*

Together, and with her continuous work on herself, that belief got unpacked piece by piece. She began to see it for what it was—a story written by someone else. It wasn't hers to carry. She redefined her values, set boundaries, and built a new truth—one where her worth was no longer tied to anyone else's opinion.

The transformation was emotional and visible. She stood taller, spoke with clarity, released relationships that drained her, and finally embraced the love and self-worth she had always deserved.

Your Turn: Get Curious About Your Narrative

Just because these beliefs have been around forever doesn't mean they get to stay. Imagine your life as a story, and you've let someone else hold the pen for far too long. Now, it's time to snatch it back and start writing the story that feels true to you.

Limiting beliefs thrive in the shadows, quietly steering your choices without you even noticing. Picture your belief as an old, dog-eared rulebook that's been sitting on a dusty shelf in your mind. You've been following it, not because it's right, but because it's *there*. It's the *only one* available. Now, it's time to blow off the dust, toss out the outdated rules, and create something new.

Step 1: Spot the Belief

What's a belief you've been carrying that feels heavy or restrictive? Maybe it's, *"I'm not smart enough,"* or *"I'll never be as good as her."* Maybe it's something that whispers, *"You're too old to start over."*

Write it down. Make it real. You can't rewrite what you don't acknowledge.

Step 2: Trace Its Roots

Where did this belief come from? Was it planted by a careless comment from a teacher? A family member's disapproval? Or something society drilled into you over time?

Be curious, not judgmental. This isn't about blaming others; it's about recognizing that this belief didn't originate with you—and it doesn't belong to you anymore.

Step 3: Feel, Don't Overthink

Ask yourself: *Does this belief feel true to me, or is it just familiar?*

Sometimes we cling to old rules simply because they're comfortable, not because they serve us. Close your eyes, take a breath, and tune in. If this belief feels heavy or suffocating, that's your sign—it's time to let it go.

Step 4: Rewrite the Rule

Now for the fun part: flip the script. Take that old belief and reframe it into something bold and empowering.

→ *Old Belief:* "I don't deserve success."
→ *New Rule:* "I define success, and I'm capable of achieving it on my terms."

Write your new rule somewhere you'll see it often. It's not just a belief—it's the first sentence of your new story.

The Power of Grace and Curiosity

Breaking free from limiting beliefs isn't about bulldozing your way to perfection—it's about being playful, curious, and gentle with yourself.

Here's the truth: you don't need to have it all figured out to begin. You just need the courage to ask, *"What if I'm wrong about this?"* and the curiosity to find out what's possible when you believe something better.

So, grab the pen. Turn the page and ask yourself: *What's the first chapter of my new story going to say?*

Chapter 2

The Secret to Happiness

I used to think happiness would arrive with fireworks—when the dream house was built, the shiny cars were parked in the driveway, the thriving career was in place, and the family portrait looked picture-perfect. All the boxes ticked in life's so-called textbook of success. It's the formula we're quietly handed by society and passed down to generations: *work hard, achieve big, live happily ever after.*

Once it's in your hands, you follow it like gospel. The message? If you tick all the boxes, you've made it.

Yet, I found myself one Tuesday afternoon, staring at the brand-new granite benchtop in the kitchen, wondering why I still felt empty. My life was built on other people's checklists!

People envied the lifestyle, the progress, the achievements. But what they couldn't see was the truth, the unfulfillment and unhappiness that stayed invisible to the naked eye.

It took courage to look deep inside me. Happiness isn't a destination or waiting for you at the end of a checklist. That 'chase-the-next-shiny-object' formula was failing.

Happiness is in the way you choose to live.
It's in the life you already have.

And most importantly, in knowing that you *have YOU.* For me, that meant breaking one of the biggest rules I'd been living by...

Unfollow the Rules: Ditching Approval

That old formula, *'work hard, achieve big, live happily ever after,'* didn't just have me chasing milestones. It had me chasing approval like my life depended on it.

Seeking approval and acknowledgment had been stitched into me for as long as I could remember. I couldn't say or do anything without needing someone to give me the green light. I didn't feel accomplished unless someone said, *"You did a great job."*

When my perfectly built world, including my role as a wife, crumbled, I realised I had to learn to rely on myself and give myself unconditional love. And that's when it hit me:

happiness couldn't be outsourced. No amount of compliments or people could fill the gap if I didn't believe in my own worth first.

Yeah, right. Easier said than done. The Mean Girl and Negative Nancy had taken up permanent residence in my head (and probably in every cell of my body), and they weren't about to give up their power easily.

The process came in waves—doubt, self-criticism, and the kind of soul-splitting self-talk that can derail you for days. But I chose to treat it like a blank canvas—one I could rebuild on, not with who I'd been told to be, but with who I was meant to become.

I had to unlearn the old ways. I had to determine my own path. I had to ditch the idea of having to prove my worth. I had to start believing I am already worthy and that I was destined for big things.

Never give anyone the power over your happiness.

This is my anchor! The moment you hand it over—to a person, a title, or a lifestyle—you're putting your peace on a leash.

Materialistic Delusion

In the quest to have it all, we lose sight of what's truly important. Telling ourselves we will be happy when we get there—when we're just trying to patch a leak with glitter tape.

Sometimes it's a new bag or a weekend getaway. Other times, it's holding onto relationships we've outgrown because letting go would mean facing the truth.

And the truth is uncomfortable. Change is hard. So we keep ourselves busy with the next distraction, avoiding the quiet moments where the real answers live.

Pause for a second and ask: *"Is this really making me happy?"*

The "big happy" isn't in your next purchase, promotion, or perfect vacation. A title won't make you feel loved. A nice top won't untangle your marriage. A new pair of shoes won't silence the critic in your head. No amount of "stuff" can make you feel safe, seen, or enough.

Without meaning, possessions are just distractions that could never replace the deep contentment that comes from within.

The next realization was the biggest milestone in my self-discovery and self-mastery journey.

What Matters

The essence of life is the relationships we build. Support, acceptance, shared joy, and unconditional love. Even then, happiness can't hinge solely on other people. Relationships shift, circumstances change, and at the end of the day, the one constant is YOU.

Real happiness blooms from the relationship you nurture with yourself.

This was one of the hardest lessons I had to learn: happiness starts with giving yourself the love and validation you seek, and doing it without drowning in guilt. For years, putting myself first felt selfish, like I was taking something away from others.

But the truth? Everyone benefits when you're fuelled. My daughters didn't lose anything when I chose to love myself—they gained a mother who had the energy and joy to truly show up for them.

Whether rich or poor, you remain the same person. What matters is how you treat others and, more importantly, how you treat yourself.

Self-trust? Inner peace? A life that feels aligned? That's the good stuff by your own definition.

Happiness is quieter and deeper than a flashy, Instagram-perfect moment:

- → It's going to bed with a smile on your face, knowing the universe has your back.
- → It's feeling content because you're strong enough to handle the lows and resilient enough to rise again.
- → It's embracing your flaws, celebrating your wins, and accepting yourself as you are, without judgment or negativity.

Happiness is knowing that you are enough, and you already have everything you need. It's your choice to notice the abundance and beauty around you.

The Happiness Challenge

Happiness is in the small, everyday choices you make.

For the next 7 days:

Morning mantra	Start the day with: *"I am enough, exactly as I am."*
Three smiles a day	Notice three moments that made you smile (a song, a text, a stranger's laugh). Write them down.
One joy, just for you	Do something tiny every day that makes *you* happy. Eat breakfast in bed. Take a walk without your phone. Wear the bold lipstick you've been hiding in the bathroom drawer.
Evening reflection	Jot down: *"What actually made me feel good today?"*

By the end of the week, you'll notice most of your real happiness came from presence, not possessions.

Closing Thoughts

Happiness is in the way you talk to yourself and how you show up for yourself. It is also sipping cappuccino in silence like it's a five-star experience. Laughing till your cheeks hurt. Seeing your children carefree and glowing with joy.

It's those ordinary moments that turn extraordinary when you're present enough to notice them.

True happiness isn't waiting somewhere out there—it's created in the now. No need to chase milestones or prove your worth. When you choose gratitude, joy, and peace, you feel aligned with the life you already have.

So the question isn't *when* you'll be happy. The question is:

Will you finally give yourself permission to claim your happiness?

Chapter 3

Love Yourself Like You Mean It

You are the only person you'll spend every single day with for the rest of your life. So why is loving yourself harder than loving anyone else?

When was the last time you genuinely said, "I love you" to yourself? For most of us, the idea feels foreign.

We work so hard to love others—partners, children, friends, parents, clients—but

rarely do we stop to think about the love we owe to ourselves.

Self-love is the foundation of everything else: emotional independence, abundance, resilience, and the freedom to truly thrive. Without it, we're like a house built on sand, trying to withstand life's storms without a steady foundation.

The Lies We've Been Told About Self-Love

We've been conditioned to think that putting ourselves first means neglecting others. That saying no makes us cold, and taking a break means we're lazy. So we never stop with our to-do lists and run on empty — paying for it with flat relationships, drained energy, and joy that feels hollow.

Believe me, I've lived like that—and I was *not* fun to be around. I was uptight, snappy, and serious, like life had been drained out of me. My only purpose seemed to be providing everything for everyone: clean house, cooked meals, perfectly folded laundry, and a smile that said, *"I've got it together,"* even when I didn't.

So no, self-love isn't selfish. It's the foundation of everything else. Without it, you're not living—you're just getting through your days and life on autopilot.

You need to show up more fully for your dreams.

A Lifetime of "Immaculate" Expectations

For years, I believed that same lie and lived by that same script. Like many women, I thought being a "good" person meant sacrificing my needs for everyone else's. I said yes when I wanted to say no. I kept the house spotless, worked tirelessly, and bent over backward to meet expectations, often voluntarily and entirely ignoring my own needs.

Self-love doesn't always begin with grand gestures—it often starts with the smallest acts of rebellion against the rules we've unknowingly followed for years.

For me, it began with a mop.

Growing up, I watched my mom juggle endless house chores while helping run my dad's business. She was unstoppable. Immaculate house? Check. Cooked breakfast, lunch, and dinner—every single day, no exceptions? Double check. Somewhere along the way, I absorbed the belief that rest was only allowed once *everything* else was done.

Fast-forward a few decades, and I became her. I scrubbed until my body ached, told myself I'd relax later, and wore my exhaustion like a badge of honour (for real! All I could talk about was what I did that day.). All this on top of running a business!

Of course, I always prioritized my girls. We did plenty of living—playing, cooking, baking, creating beautiful messes together with arts and crafts—but it had to be tidied up at the end of the day. Grumpy and tired? Oh, absolutely. On a mission to finish everything in record time? You bet.

The worst part? I'd never impose these crazy expectations on anyone else—only on myself!

When life felt overwhelming or when things weren't going my way, having a clean, organised home gave me the illusion that at least *something* was in my hands.

The Shift: From Mop to Moments

One day, mid-cleaning frenzy, I caught sight of my daughters and thought: *This isn't what I want them to remember.*

My worth wasn't tied to how clean the floors were. My mood was contagious, and not in a good way. They didn't need a mum who could win awards for spotless surfaces; they needed one who could laugh and enjoy life with them—someone present.

Letting go wasn't instant. It wasn't like I woke up one morning and threw the mop out the window. Liberation came in small, awkward steps.

Small Acts of Rebellion

Like everything else in life, it's always important to ease into the changes we are making. So I started with small things:

→ **Going for runs**—not to burn calories, but to clear my head and reclaim time for myself (even if I justified it by walking the dog).
→ **Joining an 8-week shred program** and actually cooking meals for me—not just everyone else.

→ **Saying yes to moments that mattered** and no to chores that could wait.

The world didn't stop spinning when I dropped the mop. Little by little, I started to feel the difference. My energy improved. My mood lifted. My girls valued an afternoon of fun far more than gleaming floors.

Each small act felt like reclaiming a piece of myself I'd forgotten.

I started seeking balance over perfection. My love for a clean environment still exists. I still like things tidy, but I stopped letting perfection take over my life. The old me would have felt lazy or careless for skipping a chore. It was the beginning of prioritizing more precious things in life.

Looking back, I can see my obsession with order wasn't really about cleanliness but *control*. When the bigger things in life felt unpredictable, I clung to the small things I could fix.

Cleaning gave me immediate satisfaction, but it felt shallow.

The turning point came when I began to understand that I have one life, one family, and only so many hours in a day. Slowly, that realization started to lift my perspective.

If I spent all my energy chasing impossible standards, I would miss the beautiful moments.

Making Yourself a Non-Negotiable

Once the guilt of being productive to be worthy is gone, you can start focusing on you and what makes you happy (and what doesn't). OK, we still have responsibilities, we can't just skip the school run or delete our inbox. The bills need to be paid and the laundry won't fold itself (only if kids 'volunteer'). But self-love means you don't get lost in the grind. You are just as important as everyone else around you. Be kind to yourself.

Self-love looks like (bubble baths and chocolate help, too!):

→ **Saying no without guilt.** You're allowed to protect your time and energy.

→ **Choosing rest over relentless productivity.** Rest isn't a reward; it's a necessity.

→ **Appreciating who you are,** not just what you look like.

→ **Forgiving yourself for not having it all figured out.** You're human, not a machine.

→ **Believing you are worthy of love.** Right now, as you are.

Self-love is creating space for yourself in your own life. You don't have to earn your worth—you already have it.

What belief makes you put yourself last, over and over again?

Pause and Reflect

Your story might not involve a mop, but chances are you have your own version of this: a belief that's been driving you to prioritize everything else over yourself. So, how do you begin the shift? Your Self-Love Starter Kit:

1. **Start Small:** What's one small thing you can do for yourself this week? A short walk, a quiet coffee, or even five minutes of deep breathing.

2. **Reflect:** Ask yourself – *Would I treat someone I love the way I treat myself?* If the answer is no, it's time to change the narrative.

3. **Reframe Guilt:** Remind yourself that taking care of yourself isn't selfish—it's necessary. When you're happy and healthy, you show up better for the people you love.

4. **Celebrate Small Wins:** Acknowledge each act of self-love, no matter how small. Dropping the mop for a fun afternoon counts!

Closing Thoughts

When you love yourself, you're like a deeply rooted tree—storms might sway you, but they can't break you.

No dramatic overhaul required. Just small, consistent acts of rebellion against the rules that don't serve you. Choose moments over mops, balance over perfection, and presence over pressure.

Loving yourself isn't a destination—it's a practice. Some days, it will feel easy; other days, it might feel impossible. But as long as you can love yourself, you'll get through.

Chapter 4

Guarding Your Glow with Boundaries

Oh girl, if you only knew how little boundaries I used to have, you'd send me a sympathy card. If someone made me feel uncomfortable, said something offensive, or hurt me, I stayed silent. Every single time. I felt the pressure building in my chest, the words wanting to rise, but they never came out. *I didn't have the tools.*

As a child, expressing my emotions often meant being dismissed or told off. I learned to stay quiet, to avoid conflict, and to make myself small. Speaking up felt dangerous—like the world might collapse.

Many of us grow up carrying that silence. Let people talk over us, dismiss us, and mistreat us. We tell ourselves it isn't worth the confrontation.

Deep down, all we want is to be loved, and we believe staying quiet would keep us safe.

Spoiler: It is actually the ticket to *giving up* on ourselves.

I believed it was my duty to do everything I was asked to do. If you've seen the movie *Yes Man* with Jim Carrey, I was the female version of that. I couldn't say no to anyone or anything. I was incapable. It might sound funny, but in reality, it was anything but.

While it didn't get me into trouble, it got me completely off my orbit. I wasn't living—I was existing as a puppet, waiting for people to pull the strings and tell me what to do.

Why Boundaries Seem Impossible: The Silent Struggles

I see it now in so many women around me. The hesitation in their eyes when someone crosses a line. Quietly shrinking when they're dismissed or overlooked. The stories they don't tell because they don't think they are important.

For me, the root ran deep. It wasn't just hesitation; it was paralysis. The harshness of the reactions stung me. I was unprepared for it. Every single time. I didn't see it coming, and when it hit, I froze.

The sting wasn't just in the words or actions—it was in my silence. I held back because I didn't know how to respond. I didn't have the tools or the confidence to stand up for myself. So instead, I swallowed my feelings, told myself it was ok, and wanted to disappear.

Setting boundaries feels impossible when you've been conditioned to keep the peace. It feels like sitting on a volcano, fearing the eruption that may come—upsetting someone, getting told off, and being shamed. It's not any girl's dream to feel small as a speck. It's easier to do the 'right thing': stay quiet, keep the waters calm, blend into the background. But is it worth it?

Boundaries draw a line to protect your light, energy, personal space, preferences, choices, feelings, and perspective.

Ok, I know this feels like a lot, just bear with me!

Think of boundaries as your personal bodyguard (only they don't need a lunch break or a salary), safeguarding your peace, emotions, and time, creating a reality that works for you.

Boundaries honor your worth and your energy. They are an act of self-respect.

Can they feel daunting at first? Absolutely. It's just part of the process. Setting boundaries is a *skill* you can build—one step, one moment, one 'no' at a time.

Boundaries Are Your Gift and Power

Boundaries bring clarity and respect into relationships, allowing for deeper, healthier connections.

You're protecting yourself and also teaching others how to *treat* you by setting boundaries.

They're also a gift to yourself. The kind of gift you actually want—not another scented candle you didn't ask for. They free you from the guilt of overcommitting, the resentment of being stretched too thin, and the exhaustion of trying to please everyone.

Boundaries were my game-changer. The moment I started setting them—clumsily, awkwardly, with my heart pounding in my chest—I felt a shift. I was reclaiming the voice I'd lost.

Setting boundaries doesn't have to be loud or confrontational. *It can be subtle, quiet, and deeply rooted in self-respect.* Remember, you are being *clear*, not harsh!

It wasn't easy at first. The idea of standing up for myself felt foreign and uncomfortable. That's where getting support made all the difference.

When you're new to setting boundaries, it can feel like walking through a dark room—you're unsure of where to step or how others might react. Having someone to guide you through the process, someone who isn't emotionally attached to the situation, can be invaluable. They can help you see the situation clearly, without taking sides or letting emotions cloud your judgment.

Reassurance from others who've been there can boost your confidence. Hearing, *"I've been there, and it gets easier,"* or *"You're doing the right thing,"* can be the push you need to take that first step.

With every boundary I set, I felt a little less weighed down, a little more in control. Each step was a reminder that I deserved the same respect I gave to others. The emotional relief was undeniable—like I was finally clearing space in my life to breathe, to grow, and to just *be*.

Setting boundaries takes courage.
Enforcing them takes time.

The more you do it, the more confident you become, and the easier it gets to protect yourself.

Two Types of Boundaries

Boundaries go both ways—how you deal with others and how you deal with yourself.

We overextend all the time; juggling business, family, and every role in between—designer, copywriter, accountant, customer service, chef, therapist, you name it. On top of that, we let our "Negative Nancy" (remember her from earlier?) run the show, saying things we'd never tolerate from a friend.

Internal Boundaries

These are the promises you make to yourself to safeguard your energy and well-being. They're about self-respect and self-care.

Examples:

→ "I will say 3 nice things about me today."
→ "I'll stop working at 7 p.m. to protect my rest and personal time."

78

→ "I will start with important tasks before IG notifications."

→ "I will celebrate my small wins."

External Boundaries

These are the limits you communicate and enforce with others. They're about defining what you will and won't accept in your interactions.

Examples:

→ "I'm not comfortable discussing that topic."

→ "I am unavailable for calls after 6 PM; I'll get back to you tomorrow."

→ "I need at least 24 hours' advance notice for meetings."

→ "I can only take on new projects from next month."

Ultimately, establishing both internal and external boundaries means you are crafting a framework for a more balanced, respectful, and fulfilling life, one where your energy and well-being are protected.

Closing Thoughts

At the heart of every boundary is self-worth. It's saying no when you mean no, resting without guilt, and protecting your peace.

Letting the right people in, on your terms, and preserving your energy so you can show up fully.

When you set boundaries, you are being kind to yourself and guiding others. You say yes to yourself, to your peace, and to the life you actually want. Internal boundaries stop the spiral of negative self-talk and overcommitment, while external ones show others how to respect your time, energy, and values.

Chapter 5

Unapologetically Confident

Confidence is walking into any space, from a boardroom to a first date, family gathering, or a Zoom call, *knowing exactly who you are*. Showing up authentically, trusting yourself, and embracing your flaws. Most importantly, knowing your *worth*. You don't need to be the loudest or have all the answers.

Confidence in the Micro Decisions

Confidence is shaped in the tiny, everyday promises we keep to ourselves.

The truth? When we break our promises, our confidence rarely crumbles in one big moment. It fades slowly—with every "I'll start tomorrow," every skipped commitment, every time we choose comfort and safety over courage.

After my younger daughter was born, I promised myself I'd stay active—walk, run, hit the gym. But between growing a business and solo parenting, those habits faded. Each week, I said, "Next week, I'll start again." And each week, I didn't.

Then a new gym opened in town. I toured it and felt my old spark return... until *Negative Nancy* popped up in the car park: *You're already overloaded. If you couldn't manage a workout in your home gym, what makes you think you'll show up here three times a week?*

But then came the stronger voice. "Listen, girl, this has to change. Walk into that gym **like you own the damn place!** No hesitation, no whining. Sign up. Show up. Three times a week. Period."

That decision wasn't about fitness.

It was about *confidence*—the kind that's built through the small steps we need to take every day.

The kind that says: "I've got me."

That moment reminded me what self-trust feels like. It was one small choice that shifted everything.

Maybe for you it's not the gym—it's sending that email, finally raising your prices, or having the hard conversation you've been putting off. The point is, confidence doesn't come from one grand transformation; it comes from stacking tiny moments of self-trust until you can't help but believe in yourself.

Confidence Looks Good On You

If you've ever looked up to (or even envied—no shame, as long as it fuels you) women who seem effortlessly confident, almost as if they were born that way, let me reassure you: even the most magnetic and successful women I've coached and met have had moments of doubt and hesitation.

You may feel out of your comfort zone when something new or high-stakes comes along—because that's what growth feels like. What matters is how you move through those moments.

The women who radiate confidence? They've learned to recover quickly, hold their ground, and re-center when things go wrong. The measure of true confidence isn't in the smooth sailing but in the detours, the slip-ups, and the way you own them.

Here's what that looks like in real life:

→ **The name slip-up:** You realize halfway through a presentation that you've been pronouncing the client's name wrong. Confidence is pausing, correcting yourself with a smile, and saying, "Apologies for the mix-up—let's start fresh. It's lovely to meet you properly."

→ **The coffee incident:** You spill coffee on your shirt five minutes before meeting someone important. Confidence is throwing on a jacket like it was part of the plan, and walking in unfazed. Bonus points if you own it with, "Just testing how caffeine-proof this outfit is!"

→ **The interruption:** Someone cuts you off mid-sentence. Confidence is calmly saying, "I'd like to finish my thought, and then I'd love to hear your perspective."

You can be confident and still spill your coffee or mess up a name. The magic is in how quickly you recover and keep shining.

For so long, I believed I just wasn't "one of those people" who could be confident. I thought confidence was reserved for women with perfect lives, flawless looks, and charm that could light up any room. *I was the queen of overthinking,* second-guessing every move, replaying conversations in my head, and obsessing over what others thought.

And here's the kicker: I was also validation-seeking, people-pleasing, and stuck in constant indecision. **Not sexy!** There's nothing empowering or attractive about twisting yourself into knots to keep everyone happy while losing sight of yourself.

Sexy Starts Where Insecurity Ends

So, what makes confidence magnetic?

It's not the perfect hair, the killer heels, or the skirt that says "I run this place" (although those can give you an extra spark). It's the energy you carry when you're at home in your own skin.

Here's what sexy confidence looks like:

→ **Trusting Your Decisions:** Even when they're imperfect. It's saying, *"Yes, I bought that ridiculously expensive planner because I'm convinced it will turn me into a productivity queen—and I have no regrets!"*

→ **Owning Your Flaws:** Picture yourself mid-presentation, and your slides suddenly freeze. Instead of panicking, you confidently smile and say, *"Looks like even technology needs a coffee break! No worries, this gives us a chance to discuss this point in more detail while I get it back on track."*

→ **Sharing your Story:** Think about a time you tried to launch a new service or product, and it just... fizzled. Instead of burying that memory, you might share it with other female entrepreneurs: *"I remember thinking I had the next big thing, poured my heart into it, and then... crickets. It was tough, but I learned more from that 'failure' than any success. As I always say now, 'Every misstep is just market research in disguise!'"*

→ **Showing Up Authentically:** When you walk into a room thinking, *"This is me. I may not be perfect, but I'm perfectly fine with that."*

Confidence has nothing to do with perfection. It's in your presence. It's a sense of humor, resilience, and self-respect.

Pause and Reflect

Confidence is not something you wake up with or inherit. You have to build it day by day. You train it daily like your favorite muscle (Quads for me. You?).

→ **Know Your Worth** – Your value isn't tied to your achievements or looks. Write down your strengths and keep them visible.

→ **Face Your Fears** – Do one small thing this week you've been avoiding.

→ **Speak Kindly to Yourself** – Swap *"I can't"* for *"I'm learning."*

→ **Embrace Imperfection** – Let go of getting it all right; learn as you go.

→ **Show Up Authentically** – Stop performing, start being.

Quick Confidence Boosters:

→ **The Power Pose:** Before a big meeting, event, or conversation, stand tall, take up space, and hold your head high. This small shift in body language can signal confidence to your brain.

→ **Daily Wins Tracker:** Keep a journal of your small wins each day. Over time, these add up and remind you of your progress.

→ **Confidence Visualization:** Spend five minutes each morning visualizing yourself owning the room—whether it's a real room or a metaphorical one. Picture yourself walking tall, speaking with clarity, and feeling at home in your own skin.

→ **The Red Lipstick Effect:** Whatever your version of red lipstick is—your power heels, your statement necklace, that playlist that makes you strut—wear/use it before big moments.

Closing Thoughts

I waited for the day I felt "ready". That day never came.

Confidence is born in the action.

So act before you feel ready. Take the step, even if it's messy. Walk into the room, even if you're nervous. Say yes to the opportunity, even if you doubt yourself.

At the center of every bold move is self-trust. It matters more than raw talent or credentials. Confidence is the force that turns potential into progress. It's believing that when you step into the unknown, you'll figure it out. That you'll be okay.

Confidence grows every time you stretch beyond your comfort zone and realize you're still safe. Every time you keep a promise to yourself. Every time you rise to the occasion.

Your Companion for Change

Downloadable
Workbook

Embrace what stood out or made you think in Part 2 of the book.

If you haven't already, download your **beautiful companion workbook.**

It's designed to help you
explore, embody, and make these shifts your own.

https://www.theredheelboss.com/womanizerworkbook

(or simply scan the QR Code in the image above)

Part 3: Emotional Independence – Unleashed & Untamed

"Like a lotus defying the odds to bloom in the murkiest waters, you rise—pure, resilient, and untamed. Emotional independence is about reclaiming your power, owning your story, and breaking free from the weight of expectations. This is where you find beauty in the chaos and strength in your scars, unlocking a life of boundless potential."

Chapter 1

Breaking Free from Codependency

Part 3 is about something most of us were never taught, how to become emotionally independent.

Not in a "don't need anyone" kind of way, but in the most beautiful, grounded way: where your worth, your joy, and your sense of self come from within—not from your relationship status, your job title, or how much others approve of you.

These chapters are raw, real, and sometimes a little uncomfortable. But inside them is the truth that changes everything.

Because once you stop outsourcing your power and start owning it? You become unstoppable.

Reclaiming Your Power

It took years for me to realize that the chains I wore weren't put on me by others alone. I believed they belonged to me.

For most of my life, I didn't believe I could achieve anything significant on my own. I relied on strong male figures. Their approval, their support, and, at times, even their permission dictated my every move. From choosing what I wore to deciding the trajectory of my future, I let their voices replace my own.

I don't remember exactly when it started. Maybe it wasn't just what they said or did—it was also how I learned to see myself. I thought it was normal. After all, isn't that what a "good girl" is supposed to do? She listens. She follows. She doesn't stir the waters.

Without self-worth or purpose, how could I bring my best self to any relationship?

I became small, obedient, and agreeable. I swallowed my dreams, until they became so faint I wasn't sure they'd ever existed. I didn't know how to claim what I wanted. It felt foreign, even selfish. I convinced myself that sacrificing myself was what a good partner, daughter, or mother did. And so my life became a quiet routine of service, cooking, cleaning, and making sure everyone else had what they needed—while I forgot what I needed altogether.

But then, there was that voice.

At first, it was faint, almost a figment of my imagination: *What about you?*

It came louder in the stillness of the night: *Is this the life you really want?*

And one day, the question roared like a storm inside me: *Why are you living like this?*

It was terrifying to even entertain the possibility that I can leave the life I'd always known. What if I failed? What if I wasn't capable of doing more? What if the life I had was all I deserved?

Those thoughts were paralyzing. But I knew one thing for sure: I couldn't keep living like this.

Society and Conditioning

What I experienced wasn't just personal—it was deeply rooted in the stories society tells us about how women are expected to live.

From a young age, girls are told—through words, actions, and examples—that their worth lies in being "good". To be good is to be quiet, agreeable, and self-sacrificing. It's to place others' needs ahead of your own and find fulfillment in their success. To dress and wear our hair in a certain way to be accepted and complimented.

This message seeps into every corner of our lives, shaping the choices we make, the relationships we enter, and the dreams we set aside. Even the systems we grow up in reinforce these ideas. Look at the school system: children are punished for failing as though failure is the ultimate sin.

But failure is where growth begins.

It's the birthplace of learning, stretching, and discovering what we're truly made of. Imagine if we were taught to celebrate failure—not as defeat, but as evidence of courage. Proof that we dared to try.

Instead, we're taught to fear it.

And that fear follows us into adulthood, stealing our dreams and dimming our potential.

How many times have you hesitated, second-guessed yourself, or dismissed an idea because the risk of failure felt too high? Have you avoided promotions because you doubted your worth? How about postponed hobbies, trips, and adventures, waiting for the "perfect" time?

It creeps into our businesses.

"I'm not an expert," many of my female clients say. It's so common—this instinct to shrink from acknowledging their brilliance. They dismiss their achievements, downplay their value, and lose the comparison game before they even play. There's always someone better, right?

One client of mine had 15 years of experience, two degrees, and glowing testimonials—yet she still couldn't own the word *expert*. Before we could even talk about visibility or pricing, we had to do the deeper work: rewiring those beliefs.

And in some parts of the world, that programming runs even deeper. Education is a luxury. Independence is a dream. Self-expression is impossible. Girls are raised to live in the shadows—needing permission to speak, to dream, to exist.

But this isn't just an issue women face. Men are conditioned, too, to lead, provide, protect—often at the cost of their emotional well-being. Women are told to nurture, serve, and sacrifice, often at the expense of their dreams.

This is how codependency is built: expectation by expectation, until we believe we are incomplete without someone else.

What if there is a way out? What if the first step is simply remembering who you are—before the world tells you who to be?

Reframing Failure

For years, I was terrified of what would happen if I changed my life. I thought I wouldn't make it on my own.

But I committed to one thing: I would show up every day and do my best not just for me, but for my daughters as well.

The most beautiful part? *The universe responded.* I didn't fail.

I wasn't tied to a single outcome. I just trusted that if I led with an open mind and an open heart, life would meet me halfway. And it did.

People showed up — not just clients, but soul-aligned humans who loved, accepted, and celebrated me.

Opportunities opened.

Dreams I hadn't even allowed myself to dream began to unfold.

And it all started because I was willing to risk failure and choose freedom over fear.

To trust myself, even when I had no evidence yet.

These days, I still get goosebumps when someone compliments my energy, my feminine presence, my mission... Because I remember what it took to own those things.

This is the same mindset required to run a business: Trust. Courage. Willingness to fail forward.

Pause & Reflect

Write down five moments in your life when you felt powerful and independent. This is your power list.

→ What were you doing?
→ How did it feel in your body?
→ What made that moment yours?

Now ask:

What's one thing I can do today to recreate that feeling?

This list is your proof. You *are* capable. You *are* independent. And you *can* live life on your own terms.

Chapter 2

Emotional Intelligence as Power

Emotions are powerful, but when you learn to navigate them, you hold the key to transformation—not just for yourself, but for everyone around you.

Keep Calm and... Well, It's Not That Easy

Let's get one thing straight: I've always been emotional. Joy, excitement, and enthusiasm come naturally to me. When people ask if I drink, my go-to response is: *"Add alcohol to my energy levels? Fatal mistake. You'd have to peel me off the ceiling!"* Substitutes for fun? Not needed.

But then there's the flip side—sadness, drama, and frustration. These emotions don't arrive like polite guests; they crash through the door uninvited. For years, I didn't know how to handle them. And while I'm still the kind of person who can cry a river at the smallest slight against my daughters, I've learned to regulate my emotions when it matters most. My sense of justice and fairness has only sharpened through life's trials.

But when I'm faced with a situation where I can't make it better—where I'm powerless against those who hold the control—I feel like a tiger in a cage. Pacing. Helpless. Enraged. I know it's not my place to judge or serve justice, but it still stings, *because I would never do to them what they're doing to me.* That's what makes it so hard to accept. The unfairness is in the misalignment with my own values.

Emotions aren't the enemy.
They're part of what makes us human.

They hold important messages. Grief tells us what mattered, anger shows us where our boundaries were crossed, and joy reminds us what lights us up.

The trick isn't to suppress them, but to learn how to release and express them in ways that serve your growth instead of sabotaging it.

A Tale of Two Selves: The Emotional Goddess Meets the Analytical Mind

Half of me is an accountant. She loves spreadsheets, checks reconciliations three times, and gets a thrill from organization. The other half of me? She's an emotional goddess. She feels deeply, takes pride in being a woman, and embraces the complexity of life's ups and downs.

It wasn't always this balanced. I used to hide my tears, ashamed of what they represented. Now, I see them as a cleanse—a release that clears the way for what's next.

Life has thrown me curveballs that demanded both sides of me to work together:

→ **Undergoing spinal surgery** that redefined my relationship with resilience.

→ **Moving to two foreign countries** and starting from ground zero, not once, but twice.

→ **Building seven businesses** from scratch.

→ **Running marathons**, proving endurance isn't just physical—it's mental too.

→ **Raising kids far from family support**, with no aunties or grandparents to call.

→ **Climbing the career ladder** while completing university a year early, all while working full-time.

And then there was the mother of all challenges: *securing permanent residency in New Zealand.*

The Residency Gauntlet

Picture this: I'm heavily pregnant, waddling through the chaos of bureaucracy. My then-husband's workplace had just gone into liquidation, and immigration decided to discount the points we'd earned, effectively telling us to pack up and leave.

Was I an emotional wreck? Absolutely. Did I want to collapse into tears and scream at the unfairness of it all? You bet. But there was no time for that.

The day was spent investigating, the night planning, and the next morning driving all over the city—giant pregnant belly and all. Ex-directors needed to sign validation letters, potential employers needed convincing that hiring someone days before Christmas was a brilliant idea, and immigration paperwork had to be completed and sent.

In the middle of this whirlwind, I had to call my new manager, Rex. I could have lied and called in sick, but honesty felt right. "I'm not entitled to leave yet, so I understand if this day gets deducted from my pay," I told him.

Rex, nearing retirement, was one of the kindest and most professional people I've ever met. The next day, he told me they'd decided to give me the day as paid leave. His generosity stayed with me for years. Even after I left the job post-maternity leave, we stayed in touch. Ten years later, he provided references for my applications, and we still kept in touch, updating each other on our lives.

By the end of that whirlwind day, we had pulled off what felt like a miracle. A new job offer secured, immigration documents sent, and residency saved. I sat on the edge of the bed, swollen ankles and all, clutching the paperwork like a golden ticket, wondering how on earth I'd managed to hold it all together. I hadn't just survived the storm — I had danced in it, belly and all.

Your Emotional Home

Everyone has an emotional home—a default state we return to when life gets tough. Mine used to be sadness, self-doubt, and victimhood. It was a dark, suffocating place built from years of societal conditioning and negative self-talk.

I didn't want to live there anymore. I wanted to be in control, to call the shots, to sit at the steering wheel of my life instead of being a passive passenger.

Rebuilding your emotional home is like training for a marathon: it takes discipline, determination, and the willingness to get back up after falling. You can't change your emotional home overnight, but with time, you can create a foundation that empowers you instead of holding you back. For me, shifting my emotional home changed how I made every decision from parenting to building businesses.

The Storm Before Freedom

For so many women, the decision to leave a relationship isn't a moment of empowerment—it's a breaking point.

They stay for years, living in emotional limbo. Unseen. Unheard. Unloved. Not because they're weak, *but because they're strong in all the wrong places*—shouldering pain that was never meant to be theirs, hoping love can fix what only truth can change.

Often, they feel guilty for even thinking about leaving. They take pity on their partners, empathize with their pain, and silence their own. They hear the good girl voice, *"You should be grateful. You should make it work."* And so they stay—trapped in a cycle of love, hurt, hope, repeat.

Some partners know exactly how to keep the cycle going—through charm, gaslighting, belittling, or slowly chipping away at self-trust and belief. It's hard to see clearly when you're living inside the storm. Something has to snap.

Maybe it's the realization that their children are watching, absorbing what love is *supposed* to look like.

Maybe it's the moment they wake up and feel the weight of everything they've lost—joy, freedom, identity.

Maybe it's the awareness that loneliness in peace is better than connection in pain.

I'll never know what finally prompted the barista at the petrol station (from the beginning of the book) to leave the role she described so painfully—as a housekeeper and sex slave in her own home. But I've seen it before. So many women awaken to a hard truth no one wants to face: the very basics—safety, stability, and emotional security—are missing from their lives.

Eventually, the pain outweighs the fear. And when it does, they stop settling. They stop hoping the other person will change and start remembering who they were before they were broken down.

Anything that is not love, respect, and genuine care *is a quiet crime against the human soul*.

Manifesting Abundance and Love

Like so many women who've found themselves in the quiet wreckage of a relationship that no longer feels like love, I discovered that my breakdown wasn't just in my marriage—it was in everything I thought I knew about safety, identity, and what I deserved.

But just like that little girl who once dreamed of becoming a doctor to help others and change the world, I found myself, as a grown woman, longing to change my own life. To rewrite my story. To become someone my daughters could look to and say, *"She chose light."*

Because we are not designed to stay in the darkness too long. Eventually, the desire for more becomes brighter than the fear of the unknown. And for me, that desire lit the way forward.

During that dark time, I first began fantasizing about the life I wanted, not just for survival, but for joy.

I dreamed of a love that adored every part of me, that celebrated my quirks and soaked up my words. A love that laughed off mistakes and built a foundation on trust, playfulness, and passion.

These fantasies weren't just escapism or daydreams. They were seeds. They became the foundation for something much bigger. I started manifesting abundance and peace in every area of my life. Opportunities appeared. Partnerships flourished. Clients began referring me to their friends. People began noticing something different. It wasn't just what I was saying—it was the way I carried myself. Lighter. Calmer. Grounded. Like I'd stepped into a version of me that had always been there, just waiting to be unwrapped. That emotional shift became my silent marketing tool. (More on that in Part 4!)

The universe exceeded my wildest fantasies. It was as if every small act of courage and self-belief unlocked doors I hadn't even known existed. That's when I realized I started something new and unimaginable: manifesting the life I desired!

Lessons in Emotional Intelligence

It's a misbelief that all it takes to manifest the life you desire is wishful thinking or vision boards. Manifesting physical wealth and well-being in your life requires emotional growth. Real change comes when you stop reacting to old wounds and start responding to self-awareness.

That's where emotional intelligence comes in.

It's the bridge between the pain of your past and the peace of your future.

It's the one skill they don't teach in school but should be a prerequisite to leadership, entrepreneurship, or any relationship that matters.

Because if you don't know how to handle your own emotions or navigate the emotional undercurrents of life, even the most beautiful manifestations can slip through your fingers. Learning to pause, reflect, and choose differently—that's where the real magic happens.

Here are a few tips for building emotional intelligence:

1. **Journaling for Clarity:** Writing down your thoughts helps you process emotions without judgment. Addressing issues in the third person can create the distance needed to see things clearly.
2. **Role-Playing Scenarios:** When overwhelmed, ask, *What would my ideal self do?*
3. **Focusing on Solutions:** Emotions can cloud judgment, but focusing on solutions brings clarity.

4. **The Love Approach:** Holding onto anger only weighs you down. Forgiveness isn't about excusing others—it's about freeing yourself.

Pause & Reflect

Now it's your turn:

→ What is your emotional home?

→ What small steps can you take to rebuild it?

Remember, it's not about perfection—it's about progress. Every small act of courage, every tear shed, every step forward adds to the foundation of the life you deserve.

A Final Thought

"Every master was once a disaster." You don't need to have it all figured out to begin. Just start.

Your emotions are powerful, but don't let them control you.

Navigate them with grace, and they'll become your greatest strength.

The most amazing thing regarding my two sides of emotions and organizing things is a revelation I had five months after writing this chapter. I had a soul reading with a spiritual guide and learned that my core trait is *organizing chaos*, and that's precisely why I excel at managing multiple big things simultaneously. I was absolutely fascinated to discover this was a *gift*, not a judgment, and I finally understood why this strength resonated so deeply. Because the Universe always delivers.

Chapter 3

Resilience and Resourcefulness

When things seem hopeless, and you're on the verge of giving up, remember this: the only thing that separates failure and winning is persistence.

How often have we told ourselves, *"I've tried everything"*? In those moments, it feels like we've reached the end of the road, like every possible solution has been exhausted. But the options are endless. The problem isn't that we've tried everything; it's that we've run out of steam to keep going.

The difference is taking one more step.

Just one. Because more often than not, the breakthrough is waiting just beyond the point where most people give up.

No More Survival

Every challenge we overcome builds muscle for the next one. And no, it's not always graceful—sometimes it's messy, loud, and held together with caffeine and willpower. Sometimes it looks like crying in your car between meetings or googling "how to not lose your mind" at 2 AM.

The first step is survival: doing whatever it takes to get through the day, the week, the storm.

Then, as your confidence creeps in, survival shifts into thriving—not just staying afloat, but actually enjoying the damn swim.

Eventually, thriving becomes serving: taking what nearly broke you and using it to build something meaningful, using the lessons you learned the hard way to help someone else feel a little less alone.

I used to think surviving was all I could ask for. Just get through the day, don't drop the ball, and maybe reward myself with a lukewarm cappuccino I reheated three times.

But thriving? That came the moment I stopped trying to seem perfect, polite, and Pinterest-worthy. Because honestly—who needs *another* beige, overly filtered, perfectly curated internet persona? Spoiler alert: that's how I started, and it didn't work out very well for me.

So I dropped the act. I showed up as me—showing the messy middle, rebel opinions, bold statements, and all. And you know what? My inbox started flooding with compliments like, *"You're so real,"* and *"Finally, someone who says it like it is."*

That's when it clicked: I don't need to shrink myself to be taken seriously. I don't need to sacrifice my personality, my edge, or my voice to fit into someone else's definition of "professional."

Turns out, being fully myself *is* the strategy. And honestly? It's working.

Facing Challenges: A Plan of Action

One of the bravest things I ever did was ask for help, the real kind. Not the "Can you pick up milk?" kind, but the "I'm not okay" kind. It wasn't easy, but it reassured me that I mattered. All it took was a 3 AM call, just to hear a special person's warm, sweet, cheerful voice. I was met with instant support and: "Don't worry, I've got you, girl. It happens to the best of us! You're overwhelmed because you do so much for everyone. Let's work through this!" No change of perspective of me, not thinking for a second I was weak. Telling me that I wasn't breaking, but bending to life's demands. Tuning into my soul before I picked up the phone. Intuitions are so powerful when there is a deep connection.

31 minutes of someone's time—someone amazing, who was also going through challenges yet dropped them instantly for me—was enough to pull me up from a very dark, deep place where all hope seemed lost. It was executed with the strongest, most confident energy—and with full belief in me that it was only temporary. Layered like a gourmet cheeseburger with deep, rich, and delicious sauce—unexpected, comforting, and exactly what I needed to feel whole again.

I'm beyond grateful to my closest friends and a local woman's organization for shedding light on how much I do and always reminding me of how far I've come. Knowing that they're always in my corner, watching out for me, and sensing my significant moments without words, sometimes cities or oceans away, is enough to pull me back to myself when I feel like I am drifting. Where would I be without them? My days of survival were over and I started evolving.

When life throws a challenge your way, here's how to approach it:

→ **Pause and Assess:** Take a step back. Emotions often cloud our judgment, and taking a step back from the problem can bring clarity.

→ **Break It Down:** Divide the challenge into smaller, manageable steps. Even the biggest problems can be tackled one step at a time.

→ **Focus on Solutions, Not Problems:** Instead of dwelling on what's wrong, shift your energy to what can be done to fix it.

→ **Reflect on Your Wins:** Remember the times when you've faced challenges and emerged stronger. Use those experiences as proof of your resilience.

→ **Ask for Help (this is a big one!):** Resilience doesn't mean going it alone. It takes strength to admit when you need support, whether from friends, family, or professionals.

From Exhaustion to Empowerment

Overcoming challenges is only one part of resilience. Transforming how you see yourself is the real essence. Each time you make it through a tough situation, you're proving to yourself that you're capable, resourceful, and stronger than you think.

The beauty of resilience is that it grows with every test. What once felt impossible becomes manageable. And what's manageable today will feel effortless tomorrow.

I never thought...

→ I could speak up for myself.
→ I could run two businesses in parallel—juggling deadlines, decisions, and dreams (and occasionally, takeaways).
→ I could single-handedly manage the whirlwind of teenage emotions, social calendars, "Mum, where's my...?" moments, and still keep the house standing and the wheels turning.
→ I could overcome the sting of rejection—the kind that sneaks in when you least expect it and shakes the parts of you that worked so hard to heal.

And yet, here I am.

More empowered than I've ever been.

Because what I've learned is that resilience doesn't always look like confidence or feel like progress. Sometimes, it's in the 'I'm falling apart". It's wiping your tears, resetting your alarm, and showing up anyway.

It's doing the work when nobody's watching. It's making space for yourself in a life that demands you give everything to everyone else.

It's saying, *"This is hard,"* without shame, without saying, *"I'm fine."*

Forget perfection.

Think of the small acts instead – forging through late nights, early mornings, tough conversations, and failed attempts.

You're a goddess, but not because everything's perfect or peaceful all the time. Some days, the laundry throne's overflowing, the royal court is arguing over snacks, and you're just trying to make it through without losing your mind. But still, you show up. You sort through the mess, lead with love, and somehow keep everything running. That's the kind of queen you are—the kind who runs an empire with a slightly crooked crown and gets sh*t done.

Pause & Reflect

Take a moment to think about a recent challenge you faced.

- → How did you handle it?
- → What did you learn about yourself in the process?
- → What would you do differently next time?

Write down your answers. Resilience starts with reflection, and reflection gives you the tools to handle what's next.

When you feel like giving up, remember this: the breakthrough is often just one step away.

Chapter 4

Owning Your Story

We're taught to show up polished, professional, and perfect—as if being taken seriously depends on having it all together. But you don't need to have "made it" to teach, lead, or inspire.

Some of the most powerful moments happen while we're still figuring things out. The messy middle—that place where you're growing, learning, fumbling, and showing up anyway—that's where real connection lives. That's where people relate to you. That's where your story becomes someone else's lifeline.

You don't have to wait until the ending is wrapped in a pretty bow. Your story is already enough. And so are you.

The Stories We Hide

Everyone loves a polished success story, but honestly, how often do we want to tell the *whole* story? The messy parts, the ugly cries, the mistakes that made us want to crawl under a rock and live there indefinitely?

Yeah, those stories don't usually make it to Instagram.

We all have chapters we'd rather leave out. Maybe it's the career we gave up on, the relationship that imploded, or the time we thought DIY bangs were a good idea (spoiler: they weren't). In all truth, *those messy, complicated chapters are often the ones that hold the most power.*

The parts of your story you're hiding might just be the ones that make you shine.

We are trained to sweep our struggles under the rug, slap on a smile, and present the most polished version of ourselves. Like we were weak to go through them. It's no wonder we struggle. Why?

→ **Fear of judgment:** You've started a business, and suddenly everyone's questioning how you're balancing motherhood. (*"Don't you think your kids need you more?"*)

→ **Shame:** Maybe you stayed in a toxic relationship too long or left a job everyone thought was "perfect."

→ **Expectations:** You're juggling the roles of mom, partner, professional, friend, chef, cleaner, and CEO of *Everything That Needs to Get Done, Inc.* And still, it feels like you're falling short somewhere.

I messed up plenty. And for a long time I wanted to hide those messy chapters like they didn't exist. I thought if I only showed the polished version of myself, I'd be more respected, more "together," more accepted.

But what we hide doesn't disappear. Instead, it disconnects us from others. It keeps us stuck in shame. It also keeps *them* stuck—the ones watching, silently wondering if they're the only ones still struggling.

I only started opening up about my childhood when I learned there was actually a name for it: narcissistic abuse. And when I heard that word for the first time, it hit me like a wrecking ball.

It was as if giving it a name made it even more real, more painful. Suddenly, the memories had labels. The confusion had context. And the ache I'd carried for years wasn't just "me being dramatic." It was something real. Something I survived.

It was my story. It wasn't wrapped up with a bow. But it was *true*. It gave other women permission to breathe. To speak. To heal. To be free.

People don't need your perfection. They need your humanity. They need to know it's okay to be in progress.

The messy middle is where most of us are. It's where the growth is. And when you show up from that place, you become a lighthouse — not because you've escaped the storm, but because you're still standing in it with the light on.

Telling the truth doesn't make you weak.

Finding Humor in the Hard Stuff

Don't get it twisted—owning your story doesn't mean being serious all the time. Sometimes, the most healing thing is to laugh.

Like that time I was sobbing in the car after a particularly rough day and caught my reflection in the mirror. Mascara streaks everywhere. Hair wild. I looked like a raccoon who'd just lost a fistfight.

Or the time I tried to build IKEA shelves solo—because *"how hard can it be?"* Let's just say, the result was abstract art at best. But even that taught me something: asking for help doesn't make you weak.

Humor gives you breathing room between the breakdowns and the breakthroughs.

It's the wink to yourself in the mirror, the one that says, *"You're a hot mess, babe, but you're on your way,"* that might just get you through the hardest days. Laughter doesn't erase the mess, but it can help lighten the load.

Pause & Reflect

Take a moment. Breathe. Ask yourself:

→ What part of your story have you been hiding and why?

→ What did it teach you about who you really are?

→ How might it serve as someone else's hope?

Write it down. Speak it out loud. Share it when you're ready.

A Final Thought

When you own your story, you stop waiting for permission.

You stop apologising for being too much—or not enough.

You stop shrinking.

You stand tall in your truth—unfiltered, unpolished, and *unforgettable*.

And in doing so, you don't just change your own life.

You give every woman watching you permission to do the same.

Chapter 5

Operating on High Frequencies

Your energy doesn't just follow your thoughts; it shapes your reality. When you feel whole and complete on your own, you unlock the power to attract abundance, create opportunities, and live with unshakable confidence.

The Catalyst for Emotional Independence

There's a kind of magic that comes with operating on high frequencies. Not the kind that erases problems or makes life picture-perfect. No, this magic is deeper, more profound.

You are already whole.

When you become emotionally independent, you stop outsourcing your worth. You're no longer chasing love, validation, or the next big thing. You finally understand: it all begins within.

This is where the transformation becomes complete. You're not just surviving or thriving—you're *radiating*. Your joy, presence, and energy becomes magnetic. And that's when life starts showing up for you.

The Symptoms of Low Frequencies

Operating on low frequencies? It's like trying to run through wet cement in stilettos.

Everything feels heavier. Even the smallest task turns into an emotional marathon. Work feels soul-sucking. Relationships drain you. And your dreams? They shrink into faint background noise beneath the grind.

I remember one of those days clearly: supermarket carpark, brain fog thick as soup, couldn't find my car — and suddenly that small frustration triggered an entire spiral.

What am I even doing with my life?

That's the power of low-frequency energy — it makes you question everything.

It shows up in sneaky but serious ways:

→ **In your business:** You're doing "all the right things," but none of it feels aligned or fulfilling.

→ **In your relationships:** You're always giving, rarely receiving.

→ **In your self-talk:** Doubt becomes the default setting.

The worst part? It tricks you into thinking this is just how life is. But I promise you, it doesn't have to be.

The Journey to Wholeness

I won't pretend this shift is easy. It takes intention, healing, and a big ol' dose of unlearning.

My journey started with small, rebellious acts of self-care. A bath. A solo walk. Five minutes with my thoughts and a warm drink. Not glamorous, but powerful.

Of course, reality had other plans.

Picture this: I finally slide into the tub, candles lit, Spotify humming, and then — *knock knock* — "Muuuuum! It's an emergency!" (Spoiler: it's not.)

Or I sit down with my perfect cappuccino... only for my dog to lose her mind, charging at some imaginary intruder. Goodbye coffee. Hello chaos.

But those moments still count. Every time I choose to honor my needs, no matter how small, I am telling the universe: *I'm worth it.*

And the universe listens.

Shifting Mindset and Energy

Let's call it what it is:

The energy you put out is the energy you get back.

When I was swimming in fear, scarcity, and self-doubt, life mirrored that right back to me. But when I decided to shift?

→ **Gratitude became my default:** Even on rough days, I trained my brain to notice what was *still good*.

→ **Abundance replaced scarcity:** I stopped clutching to the idea that there's "not enough" — and trusted what I needed would arrive.

→ **Confidence replaced self-doubt:** I started making decisions as the woman I *wanted* to become, not the one who I used to be.

Practical Steps to Shift Your Frequency

Let's ground this in action.

1. **Reclaim Your Energy:** Say "no" more often—even to that tempting project or person if it doesn't feel right. Especially then!
2. **Practice Gratitude Daily:** Write down three things you're grateful for every day. Watch your mindset (and life) shift.
3. **Visualize Your Highest Self:** Who is she? How does she move? Speak? Choose? Start becoming her in micro-moments.
4. **Surround Yourself with High-Frequency People:** You become who you're around. Seek energy expanders — not drainers.

5. **Celebrate Small Wins:** Every time you respect your boundaries, your truth, or your time — that's a win. That's the new standard.

Real Talk: Not long ago, I turned down a potential client. They were pushy, chaotic, and wanted quick results without commitment. The old me would've taken the job to please, to prove myself, to chase the income.

But I said no.

They stared at me like I'd grown two heads—and maybe I had. Maybe I was finally becoming the woman who values peace over people-pleasing. Who understands that

aligned energy is more profitable than any rushed paycheck.

That, right there, is how you raise your frequency.

When the Universe Winks (and Delivers Your Groceries)

Living in alignment doesn't always look magical... until it *does.*

Years ago, I was trudging home, grocery bags slicing into my hands like plastic guillotines. I had no car, no help, and probably overestimated how much I could carry. Of course.

Just when I was ready to cry on the pavement, a car turned around and a woman offered me a ride. "You looked like you needed help," she smiled.

I almost climbed into the backseat like a kidnapped potato sack, I was so grateful.

Little moment? Yes.

Massive sign? Absolutely.

Alignment feels like that. Like tiny miracles showing up when you least expect them.

Abundance on the Path Less Taken

Over the last few years, I've manifested what once felt impossible:

→ Soul-aligned clients and collaborators
→ Deep friendships rooted in love, not performance
→ Opportunities that feel hand-delivered by the universe
→ And one chilly morning walk that gave me the sign I never saw coming

I was out with Miss Panda, walking a quiet trail no one ever uses. The sun lit up the frost like glitter. The air was still. I felt grounded, connected.

Then I turned around.

On the ground, a crisp $50 note. Just sitting there. No one around.

I didn't just see cash — I saw a message:

Abundance is on its way.

Not because I chased it.

But because I'm finally *ready* to receive it.

The signs didn't stop there.

Lately, the Universe has been speaking to me through the most unexpected channels. One moment I'm watching a film, the next I'm Googling something seemingly random... and suddenly, I've landed on a destination so deeply personal, so eerily aligned with my dreams and my future, that I have to *pinch myself* to believe it's real.

Some people call it coincidence.

I call it guidance.

That's the feeling of alignment—unexpected, thrilling, and a clear sign the universe is winking at you. When you operate on these higher frequencies, you become genuinely **magnetic**. You attract what you need not because you're desperately chasing it, but because you're finally ready to receive it.

A Final Thought

You don't need to do more. You need to *align more.*

You don't need to earn your worth. You just need to remember it.

When you operate on high frequencies, you don't hustle for what you want, you attract it. You embody it.

This chapter isn't an encouragement to ignore hard things but to meet them with a new kind of energy of trust and joy.

The power is already within you.

It's time to turn it all the way up.

Your Companion for Change

Hey beautiful. Treat yourself with this
beautiful companion workbook.

The matching pages for Part 3 are created to guide you in turning these ideas into meaningful daily practices.

Download it here:

https://www.theredheelboss.com/womanizerworkbook

(or simply scan the QR Code in the image above)

Part 4: Financial Freedom – Unstoppable & Unlimited

"Like the orchid, you are a force of resilience and elegance, thriving in unexpected places and blooming with unapologetic beauty. Financial freedom is far more than just money! It is the freedom to create, live, and lead on your own terms. This is where your power expands, your potential becomes limitless, and your legacy begins."

Chapter 1

The Wealth We Were Never Taught to Claim

You can't build financial freedom on a foundation made of other people's fears, limitations, and expectations.

First, you have to unlearn the version of yourself the world told you to be.

In the previous chapters, you've:

- → done the inner work
- → faced the stories, the shame, and the silence
- → ripped off the mask
- → reconnected with your power
- → redefined your worth — no longer tying it to roles, achievements, or approval
- → reclaimed your voice
- → remembered what's yours to claim

Now it's time to *use it*.

No more chasing money for approval or proving your worth. You already know you're worthy.

You can start honoring your freedom, building your empire, and never settling for scraps again.

You're here to break rules, build wealth, and lead your life your way.

Let's go!

What Wealth Really Means — And Who It's For

For centuries, the notion of women and money has been fraught with limitations, myths, and societal norms that have placed us on the sidelines of financial freedom. We were taught to manage money but not to create it. To stretch every dollar but not to question why it wasn't ours to begin with.

Is this just about money? Hell no. This is about power, purpose, and finally having a say in how your life unfolds. *This is the era of women stepping into their power, rewriting the story of what's possible, and redefining what wealth truly means.* Women forge the path in leading with heart and building businesses that not only support our dreams but also shape a better future for others.

Wealth isn't meant to be accumulating zeros alone.

Real financial freedom also means creating a life that feels aligned with your values, passions, and purpose.

It's the freedom to shape your days around what you love—whether that's spending more time with your family, diving into a passion project, or simply reclaiming your time.

Imagine walking into a store you've always admired and making it your favorite! Booking that trip without blinking at the cost of the flight. Knowing that your time—your most valuable resource—is entirely yours to spend on things to enjoy.

It's time to debunk the old conditioning and beliefs that wealth is simply a number in a bank account or worse, that it's something reserved for the fortunate.

It's stepping into your full potential and reclaiming your right to live a life of freedom and abundance.

From Quiet Managers to Bold Earners

I learned firsthand how contradictory society's messaging about money could be at a young age.

Growing up, my father ran his very profitable stone masonry business from home. A business he had been running before I was even born. People came from faraway towns and villages to him, as he had a great reputation. Our property was big enough to accommodate his workshop in the backyard and his office in our living room. Later on, when the business expanded, he moved to a large workshop and premises two streets away (which, by the way, our family dog absolutely disapproved of — she kept escaping through the fence to get back home!). But back then, home was where it all happened, and I got a front-row seat to watch it operate.

I vividly remember the elderly ladies coming to pay him in cash (this was waaaay before online banking, mind you!). They'd hand him stacks of dollar notes, and to my surprise, he gave me the task of counting the money.

And let me tell you, it wasn't pocket change. It was a lot of money. *Yet he trusted me with it.* Me, a teenage girl! There I was, barely a teenager, counting stacks of cash like a pint-sized CEO—high on responsibility, low on height, but totally in my element. I sat there, carefully counting every bill, feeling like I was part of something significant.

But while I was allowed to count the money, the idea of ME earning that kind of money myself? That wasn't even a conversation. It wasn't discouraged outright; it just didn't exist. The unspoken rule was clear: men earned the money, and women managed it.

How can this contradiction exist in society? On one hand, women are expected to handle family budgets, track expenses, and allocate money for everything—from college funds and groceries to family holidays, car leases, mortgage repayments, you name it. We're the financial managers of the household. But when it comes to earning money? Suddenly, the narrative shifts: "Women aren't good with money," or "It's not their role to earn."

Seriously? We're trusted to balance the entire household's cash flow but not to generate income ourselves!? This contradiction runs deep.

Money and women? **TABOO!** We're allowed to manage the household budget — just not the million-dollar decisions. It's time to break that, wouldn't you agree?

When we step into roles as earners and creators, we bring empathy, collaboration, and vision to the table. These qualities make us uniquely suited to thrive as leaders and entrepreneurs. We don't just build wealth; we build legacies. We nurture communities, create opportunities, and inspire others to dream bigger.

The Most Important Question

So, what does it feel like when your finances work for you instead of against you?

It feels like *freedom*. Like having control over your time, your choices, and your life. It's having your own bank account—no questions asked if you decide to treat yourself to a spa day or splurge on something that lights you up. It's being able to spoil your kids, take that spontaneous trip, or say yes to the little luxuries *without guilt or permission*. That's wealth. It's the ability to say no to what doesn't serve you and yes to what lights you up.

It's living on your own terms, unapologetically.

There is only one problem. While financial freedom feels liberating, so many of us are stuck believing it's out of reach. Maybe it's the conditioning we grew up with, or maybe it's the constant comparisons we make. The highlight reels of social media aren't exactly helping.

Scroll-Stopping Reality Checks

Let's talk about the *real* wealth gap—the one between our actual lives and the curated fantasies we see on Instagram.

In about ten minutes of scrolling, you're hit with

- → A tropical holiday in the Maldives,
- → Someone's kid getting a gold star for using the potty
- → A girls' weekend with spa treatments that cost more than your rent
- → An influencer showing off their *"I made six figures in my sleep"* reel
- → A shiny Lamborghini parked outside a mansion
- → Someone lounging in a palace so enormous it probably has its own zip code

Meanwhile, you're trying to decide whether the generic or big-brand cereal is a better deal this week.

It's all very mesmerizing. Some of it is downright unrealistic (seriously, who even *needs* a bathtub full of rose petals?). Yet, somehow, there we are, staring at our screens, feeling like a nobody who has accomplished nothing.

Mimicking what you see online is tempting, but financial freedom is about defining success on your terms, acknowledging what truly matters to you, and taking the steps to build that life, not the Instagram version of it.

Here's what they don't show on Instagram:

→ The woman who stayed up until midnight finishing a project when her kids were finally asleep.

→ The mom who talked her toddler out of a meltdown in the cereal aisle like a hostage negotiator.

→ The solopreneur who hit "publish" on her website even though her hands were shaking.

These are the real victories. The quiet, unseen moments where strength and resilience shine. And guess what? You're already showing up every single day. For work, for your family, for your community. You juggle endless responsibilities, solve problems that no one notices, and ensure everyone is taken care of.

But how about your dreams you haven't yet had the time, energy, or courage to chase?

What if you could turn that energy from the scroll toward your financial freedom? Instead of letting social media be a place where you compare, despair, and feel small, why not use it as a tool? Why not let it inspire you to create a life that aligns with your true goals?

The journey to financial freedom is progress, not perfection!

So let's celebrate your wins, no matter how small, and recognize that every step you take gets you closer to the life you deserve.

Owning Your Financial Story

We've been taught to see wealth as something distant, unattainable, and reserved for others. For centuries, societal norms have placed us in the background, quietly managing household finances while the bold earning was left to someone else. But what if we stopped playing small?

Financial freedom is your opportunity to *rewrite that story*. Remember that teenage girl counting cash in the living room? She didn't just learn how to manage money—she got her first taste of power. And now?

She's ready to run the show.

It feels liberating to step into the driver's seat, claim your power, and build a life that aligns with your dreams. Whether it's leaving behind the comparison trap of social media or redefining success on your own terms, this journey is deeply personal — and entirely possible.

You've been managing so much already. Imagine channeling that energy, resourcefulness, and determination into creating wealth for yourself and your family. Imagine waking up to a life where you call the shots — where your dreams are no longer on the back burner.

Every quiet victory, every step forward brings you closer to claiming the wealth that was always within your reach. The kind of wealth that doesn't just add zeros to a bank account but adds joy, freedom, and purpose to your life.

Pause & Reflect

1. **Your Personal Definition of Wealth**
   Write down your definition of financial freedom. How does it align with your current life? What changes would you need to make to feel like you're living authentically?
2. **Freedom Wishlist**
   Make a list of three ways financial freedom could transform your life. Think about time, location, relationships, and experiences— what would your days look like?

3. **Bonus Challenge: Post Your Own Highlight Reel**

   Take a moment to share one thing you've achieved recently, big or small, that makes you proud. Own your success and celebrate it, even if it doesn't look like a luxury vacation or a shiny new car.

What does your rich life *look* like — emotionally, spiritually, socially?

Don't forget to tag @theredheelboss.

Closing Thoughts

Financial freedom is *not* about recreating someone else's life!

It's a foundation for living authentically, with time, freedom, and alignment. It's breaking free from the rules and expectations that keep you small and stepping into a life that feels *uniquely yours.*

It gives you the option to *build your own*. Learning to turn inward, define your values, and align your actions with your goals. Every small step you take, every quiet victory you celebrate, brings you closer to living life on your own terms.

This is your wake-up call to *start thinking bigger*, to *believe* that your version of freedom is waiting for you. Because here's the truth: you don't have to wait for permission or a perfect plan. You've had the power all along; it's time to use it, *it's time you own it.*

Chapter 2

Healing Your Relationship with Money

Money has been labelled evil, blamed for changing personalities and ruining lives. False!

Money is neutral.

Paper. Metal. Numbers on a screen.

It has no agenda till it lands in someone's hands. That's when its true character shows, because money doesn't *change, only reveals* who you are. *It magnifies your intentions.*

Good people do incredible things with it. Selfish people do selfish things with it.

And those too afraid to claim it? Often stay stuck in survival mode.

Money isn't the problem. It's the beliefs we've inherited around it that cause the real damage.

Why We Fear Money

For many of us, money is the cause of tension, not celebration. It creates stress, not safety. And what we witness shapes what we believe — often without us even realizing it.

We're told money is hard to earn. That it slips through fingers faster than it lands. That you have to trade exhaustion for income — and that wanting more makes you ungrateful.

Sound familiar?

- → "Money doesn't grow on trees."
- → "Money is hard to come by."
- → "You have to work hard."
- → "Rich people are selfish."
- → "We can't get rich."

Maybe you grew up hearing things like "we can't afford that," or watched your parents stress over bills, or were told not to expect too much out of life. These childhood experiences, parental role models, and societal narratives stick. Over time, they create limiting beliefs.

We develop a fear of money as most of us weren't taught to love, respect, or understand money. We were taught to fear it, to chase it, or to feel guilty about it.

These early experiences carve deep grooves in our subconscious, silently influencing how we see money today.

Reprogramming the Subconscious

What you think about money runs your life.

Did you know that around 85% of your financial decisions are driven by your subconscious mind? This means most of your beliefs about money — how much you deserve, how you should earn it, and how you should spend it — are on autopilot.

If you believe money is "hard to get" or "evil," you'll subconsciously sabotage opportunities for abundance. Those outdated beliefs become invisible barriers that hold you back.

These subconscious scripts limit how much wealth you feel comfortable attracting and keeping (yes, the spending it ALL is real!).

How to Rewrite the Script:

→ Awareness: Identify and write down the beliefs you learned about money growing up.

→ Challenge Them: Ask yourself, "Is this belief true? Where did it come from? Does it still serve me?"

→ Reframe Them: Replace outdated beliefs with empowering ones. Example: "Money is abundant, and I am worthy of wealth."

Claiming Financial Power

Women who claim their financial power open doors for their daughters, sisters, and communities. This is far beyond stacking up money. It helps reclaim autonomy and rewrite outdated rules.

Let me share an example.

During a recent Rescue Mentoring Session, I worked with a coach whose pricing didn't reflect the value of her work. She was undercharging, barely covering her time, let alone the extensive preparation and follow-up she provided. After redefining her niche, her services were aligned, and her business got restructured into a three-month package delivering longer-lasting outcomes. This is the blueprint to increase income and confidence!

The lesson? When you value yourself, others do, too.

This isn't just about one woman. Across the globe, women are rising as financial leaders. From entrepreneurs in developing countries fighting for funding to CEOs breaking glass ceilings, the journey is hard-fought — and worth every step.

Still, many women—especially those helping in family businesses—do it unpaid. They handle customer service, admin, and accounting, often without recognition or payment. Others hide beauty appointments or shopping spends from their partners in fear of disapproval. It's the truth we live. And it's time we talk about it!

And the men who already champion their partners' autonomy—who cheer the facial, the MBA, the dream—they understand and shake their heads. We see you, and we thank you for being part of the revolution.

It should be normalized by everyone that women have their own income and bank account without having to justify where every dollar goes! It's not retail therapy. It's *independence,* being in control of your life and your choices, and treating yourself or supporting others without approval.

It feels like freedom. Like having control over your time, your choices, and your life. It's the ability to say no to what doesn't serve you and yes to what lights you up. To go to the beautician without guilt. To buy gifts for your children without asking permission. To be the teenage girl I once was, secretly counting cash in her sock drawer, hoping to have *just enough* to buy her own freedom one day.

This is the real glow-up.

The Feminine Energy of Money

Money is a relationship — and you can't attract what you resent.

Most women approach money with fear, guilt, or detachment. But money thrives on the same things any healthy relationship does: trust, gratitude, and care.

Once a good relationship is built with money, women naturally bring a unique energy to it — one of nurturing, connection, and purpose. Money is a resource that allows us to build, create, and grow.

Celebrate your divine, feminine energy that thrives on trust, collaboration, and intuition. Making empowered financial decisions that align with your values is one of the most radical acts of rebellion there is.

Practical ways to tap into feminine energy around money:

→ **Gratitude:** Regularly acknowledge and celebrate the money you already have.

→ **Purpose:** Define *why* you want wealth. For your family? Your future? Your freedom?

→ **Flow:** Let go of rigidity. Like a healthy relationship, money thrives in give and take.

A fitness guru I admire embodies this beautifully. She shares her income transparently, treats her team like family, and gives generously — not because she *should*, but because it brings her joy. She even bought a car for her housekeeper. That's not something every employer would do!

She also talks about taboo things like her cosmetic procedures, saying, "You make the money, you make the rules." It's a whole vibe. And it's a reminder: money doesn't change you — it reveals you.

Money Talks... Making Your Wishes Come True

Money opens doors to health, education, and experiences. It gives you options — and options are freedom.

Think about health. With money, you can afford preventative care, access the best treatments, and recover faster. Without it, you're left with fewer choices and more stress.

Money also creates memories. My travels with my daughters — from tropical beaches and swimming with sharks to finding local gems — are moments we'll treasure forever. They're the fabric of our bond. Priceless. And only possible because of financial freedom.

But I've also seen the other side. A couple I knew ran a highly profitable business but barely lived. They hoarded their wealth, never traveled, and rarely treated themselves. They were rich on paper but missed out on joy.

Money doesn't make you happy — but it lets you create a life that does.

So the question isn't *how much* you have. The question is, *what will you do with it?*

Pause & Reflect

Gratitude Journal: List 5 things money allowed you to do or experience recently. Gratitude is the gateway to abundance.

Affirmations for Abundance:

→ "I deserve to be wealthy, happy, and free."

→ "Money flows to me with ease, and I use it wisely and purposefully."

→ "I am worthy of financial abundance, and I attract it effortlessly."

→ "I love money, and money loves me." Write them. Say them. Live them.

Closing Thoughts

You weren't born to beg, budget, or barely get by.

You were born to build, receive, and lead.

To make money on your terms — with values, vision, and unapologetic power.

It reflects your self-worth, your boundaries, and your dreams.

The more love, trust, and purpose you bring into it, the more it brings back to you.

Your next level of abundance?

It starts with you.

Chapter 3

You Are Worth More Than a Million Bucks

Your worth isn't up for debate. We're just going to build a life and a business that finally reflects it.

Money Can't Define You

Money alone doesn't define your value. It's a tool, a resource, and a vehicle to create freedom, opportunity, and impact. Your worth? Already installed. Build your life based on your values, contentment, gratitude, and self-belief—the kind of things money can't buy and no one can take away.

You are worth more than a million bucks, no matter what's in your bank account. But here's the kicker—when you recognize your worth, you start treating money differently. It stops being a verdict and starts being a key.

A key to freedom, choices, and experiences.

Yet so many of us negotiate against ourselves, discount preemptively, and feel weird when someone actually wants to pay us. (Hi, it's me. I negotiated against myself so hard I nearly sent a client an invoice for zero *and* a thank-you gift.) Many women believe they should not be charging for their services as they are not an expert, don't have qualifications, haven't been doing it long enough, etc.

If you've ever thought, *"If only I had more money, I'd finally feel secure, confident, or happy"*... that's a lie we were sold. Money opens doors, but *you* decide who walks through and why. This chapter is about anchoring your worth so money can play the role it's meant to: fuel, not identity.

A Family Legacy: Building From Scratch

I'm a third-generation entrepreneur. Our legacy wasn't paved with gold—it was paved with pride, resilience, and more than a few moments of sheer determination. Let me take you back.

Granddad & the Watermelons

My grandfather was a farmer and his watermelons were legendary. First stall to sell out at the market—every time. Yes, they were sweet and unbelievably oversized, but his real edge was him: straightforward, honest, caring. People trusted him. Then life hit: betrayals, and a vineyard gone overnight when the government took it. He didn't crumble. He recalibrated. His unspoken motto: provide for your family, no matter what.

My Father, the Stone Mason

In the 1960s—long before websites and Canva—my dad decided he'd never work for anyone else. He built a thriving stone masonry business on craftsmanship and warmth. Clients returned for the quality; they stayed because they liked him for his warmth and charisma. He had a way of making everyone feel like family—clients included.

Family role call? Oh, we worked. I learned to brush gold leaf into carved letters on granite, fill hairline gaps, and come home with granite dust in places dust should never be. Some kids had lemonade stands; I had a steady hand and a sense of pride.

Those early lessons stuck: honor the details, lead with integrity, and never be too important to roll up your sleeves.

Me: The Rebel Entrepreneur

Fast forward to me, the third generation. No one was expecting the girl to run the show. Surprise: I did. Not with headstones or melons, but with creativity. Entrepreneurship was in my blood after all.

I started by sewing personalized cushions and aprons for my girls. The next thing I knew, friends were asking for their own. Orders snowballed. Soon it was Christmas runners, coasters, cushions, markets... and then? I took over the market itself. It was on life support; I gave it CPR and grew it into a 2,000-vendor operation across multiple locations.

Not bad for a girl who once doubted her ability to run her own business.

From Scarcity to Abundance

I might have given you the wrong impression, though. My business adventures have been far from straightforward and easy. Even with the legacy and evidence, I still undervalued myself. I negotiated against myself so often I practically put myself on clearance. Charging what I was worth felt... uncomfortable. Being well-paid felt... unfamiliar.

It took years to realize that **self-worth isn't measured by a number**; instead, it blossoms from *alignment, trust, and truly showing up for yourself.* When you show up as the real you—self-trust, self-respect, self-belief—your prices stop feeling scary and start feeling accurate. Your worth blooms like a many-petaled flower: each petal a practice—boundaries, voice, standards, discernment.

And once you're in alignment? The world responds. Opportunities recognize you because *you* recognize you.

The Million-Dollar Mindset

A million-dollar mindset is simply the way you carry yourself before the money shows up. It's knowing you're valuable *now* and making choices that match. How you carry yourself *everywhere*—in your business, your relationships, your health, your creativity—not just your bank app. It's knowing you're valuable now and making choices that match: clear yeses, clean boundaries, brave asks, and course-corrections without the drama. Less proving, more providing. Less hustle to be chosen, more leading like you already are.

It's calm, clear, grounded, generous, curious, and a little rebellious. You trust your voice, protect your energy, and let joy fuel your work. You say what you charge without a TED Talk. You meet problems with, "Okay—what's the next smart move?" and you keep showing up, even when it's messy.

You believe you are worthy before the results.

What it looks like in real life:

- → "The investment is $X." (full stop—no nervous discounting)
- → Choosing clients who respect your boundaries—and letting the rest go
- → Posting the 80% version instead of waiting for perfect
- → Asking for the intro, the collab, the stage—today, not "someday"
- → Paying yourself first and checking your numbers weekly (no money-avoidance)
- → Packaging your work so results—not hours—lead the price
- → Receiving compliments and cash with "Thank you—I'm proud of this"

That's the vibe. Decide, price, protect, show up. Do that consistently—and the money becomes the receipt for how you already think.

Pause & Reflect

Make Your Worth Visible (Toolkit)!

Purpose: Look beyond money metrics so you can see and show your real value.

Do this:

1. **List 3 non-money assets** that make you undeniable (e.g., resilience under pressure, ability to simplify complex ideas, community-building, creative problem-solving, emotional intelligence).

2. **For each asset, choose one action this week** that puts it on display.

→	Resilience	Share a behind-the-scenes "kept going" story.
→	Simplifier	Post a 5-step mini-framework.
→	Community-builder	Host a 20-min live Q&A.
→	Emotional intelligence	Write a client case study focusing on care + results.

3. **Capture a receipt** (screenshot, testimonial, metric) to add to your "Worth Folder."

Why it matters: When you make your non-money value visible as an act of self-respect, the money tends to follow.

Finishing Thoughts

My family's three generations of entrepreneurship taught me that real wealth is found beyond zeros; in resilience, reinvention, and the courage to keep going. When you heal your money story, you stop chasing from *lack* and start building from *worth*. Your true currencies are confidence, self-respect, and your authentic story.

Stand there, and you become magnetic. Opportunities, the right clients, and the right money find you. You're not just building a business; you're building a legacy that lives beyond any price tag.

Chapter 4

Manifesting Abundance: The Inner Work of Success

Manifestation is one of the most misunderstood topics. Affirmations and vision boards are cute—dealbreakers they are not. The missing ingredient? *Belief* so real your whole being stands behind it and recognizes it as true... so true your breath softens, your shoulders drop, and the next step feels not dramatic, but obvious.

You can't "convince" your brain you're a soon-to-be millionaire when your bank account is flat and there's no path in sight. You can't call in a life you can't *feel* yourself living or explain what you'd actually do once you got there. And if you don't know your **why**, your nervous system hits the brakes and everything stays exactly the same.

Change nothing...and nothing changes.

We're going to connect your past to your present, and bring your future **into** today—so your beliefs and your behavior finally point in the same direction.

Connecting Manifestation to You

Manifestation only works when your *beliefs* and your *body* agree. Translation: your nervous system has to recognize your next level as safe and doable—not a cinematic fantasy that spikes your anxiety.

Think of money as energy that follows direction. Your beliefs set the filter for what you notice, what you try, and what you allow yourself to receive.

Decide you want a red Mercedes and suddenly you see red Mercedes everywhere. The world didn't change—*your attention did.* The same happens with clients, opportunities, and money: get clear (and honest) about what you want, and doors you'd missed start appearing.

Make the next step that feels aligned. Big leaps read well on Instagram but real progress feels steady in your chest and quiet in your jaw. Prioritize changes small enough to practice daily and solid enough to hold.

"I'm stuck"	"I can create **$1K months** again."
"$1K feels solid"	"I'm learning **consistent $5K months**."
"$5K is normal"	"**$10K months** are my new baseline."

Not "I'm a millionaire by Friday," but "Today I will show up as a woman whose work is worth paying for—and I'll do it again tomorrow."

Future-Me cue: before any choice, ask:

> *"What would Future Me choose?"*

Then do the smallest thing now. Send the email, post the offer, name the price.

Feel It to Make It Real

You won't get a million dropped in your lap for wishful thinking. Momentum happens when you connect past lessons, present gratitude, and a future you can actually feel.

This is the emotional calibration that makes your next level feel **familiar** instead of foreign.

Past: take the lesson, ditch the leash

You can't edit history, but you can choose its job description. Let it train you—not chain you.

One-liner to write today:

"Because ___ happened, I'm better at ___ now."

(E.g., Because that launch flopped, I'm better at asking for feedback.)

Present: gratitude as grounding

Gratitude doesn't live in Pinterest quotes. Gratitude helps you be in the present and regulates your nervous system so growth feels safe. When you truly appreciate what you already have instead of taking it for granted, you create energy for positivity and abundance to flow effortlessly. It can be your beautiful home, fresh water in the tap, your health, or cherished relationships.

Do your **Daily 3**: one health win (slept 7 hours), one relationship win (sent a thank-you), one money win (paid the bill, saved $20, closed a sale).

This shifts you from "never enough" to "look what I can build on."

Future: five-sense rehearsal

The future is where your boldest dreams live. Ask your higher power—God, the Universe, the Source—clearly for what you want, and always leave room for *"or something better."* Your imagination is shaped by your past; your higher power isn't.

Now grow into it by acting like the woman you're becoming **today**.

What would Million-Dollar You do, say, wear, decide?

How would she set prices, answer emails, protect her time?

When you embody that energy now, life starts arranging around it.

Make it familiar (2–3 minutes):

- → **See:** a spacious calendar, a simple offer suite, an inbox with a "you changed my life" note.
- → **Hear:** the clean *ping* of a payment; your steady voice saying, "The investment is $_____."
- → **Smell/Taste:** your morning coffee as you open your money tracker.
- → **Feel:** shoulders lowered at 3 p.m., choices made without wobble, nervous system calm.

Emotional Mapping (Make It Stick)

Alignment comes through practice, it won't be an overnight flip. Emotional mapping teaches your brain and body to tag your biggest goals as *safe and achievable*—not distant movie scenes. You rehearse the **feeling** of already having what you want, so your system stops bracing and starts allowing. That's how you bridge the gap between where you are and where you're headed.

It's a core tool I guide students through in my Feminine Energy & Business Mastery programs—a simple practice you can return to for life: feel it first, then follow it with action.

Pause & Reflect

Tiny, doable actions to empower your journey and put this into practice:

Define Your North Star (5 min)

"I am creating _____ so that _____." (Make it about freedom, not optics.)

Past/Present/Future Sweep (10 min)

- → *Past:* one story I'm releasing one lesson I'm keeping.

→ *Present:* five gratitudes (health, people, skills, money, self).

→ *Future:* three actions Future-Me would take this week.

Belief Reframe (3 min)

→ Old: "I'm not good with money."

→ New: "I'm learning to lead money—clearly, calmly, consistently."

Five-Sense Scene Script (4 min)

Write a mini-scene from a normal day in your next-level life—coffee, tone of your emails, client joy, bank app, a 3 p.m. walk without panic. Read it each morning; take one matching action.

One Brave Ask (2 min)

Send the message right now: the intro, the collab, the raise, the sale. Closed mouths don't get fed.

Closing Thoughts

Your path is yours. Messy, magical, unmistakably you. The child who wanted to heal and the woman who's building a business? Same heartbeat. Manifestation is a daily practice of choosing yourself: asking boldly, honoring your values, and letting more good in.

Keep moving. Keep receiving.

Chapter 5

Brand Your Brilliance: Unlock Financial Freedom

You've done the inner work. You've rebuilt your beliefs. Now it's time for the outside to catch up.

This chapter turns identity into income by helping you show up in full authenticity, with a clear voice, and the confidence to attract right-fit clients, premium opportunities, and sustainable income.

Abundance from the Inside Out

They told me financial freedom was about numbers in a bank account.

They were wrong.

True freedom is waking up knowing you can make money in a way that lights you up, feels aligned, purposeful, and easy, without selling your soul or your sanity.

And the fastest way to get there? Your personal brand. It's the mirror of your truth, values, vision, and mission. The world sees *you*, and the right people feel drawn to be and work with you.

It's like walking into a crowded room and, without saying a word or wearing the brightest dress, people sense your presence and energy. You don't have to shout to be seen—you simply *are* seen.

Your personal brand is also a lighthouse—standing tall, shining steadily, guiding the right people to your shore while the wrong ones sail on by.

When you align who you are on the inside with what you show the world, your brand becomes a magnet—not just for clients, but for the life you've been manifesting all along. The kind of life where opportunities feel like they've been waiting for you, and abundance shows up without the hustle or proving your worth.

In previous chapters, we peeled back the layers of our relationship with money, redefined wealth beyond mere dollar notes, and explored the power of manifestation as a bridge between our desires and reality.

We've already peeled back money myths, reclaimed self-worth, and learned how to align belief with action. Now we bring it all together. Your personal brand is the **vehicle** that turns inner certainty into outer abundance.

Red Carpet Dreams, Wobbly Heels, and a Wake-Up Call

There I was, trembling in my high heels, feeling like the world was watching and judging me, and some were. I didn't know how I'd make it work with the odds stacked, the resistance loud, and my own doubts louder. But one thing I knew for sure: I was going to damn try, even though for the moment all I had was to hang onto my dream. The vision had me by the collar. It wasn't just a daydream or fantasy. It felt like it was assigned to me and inked into my bones like a contract.

My job? Be the voice for the women who didn't yet have the courage to stand tall, have the strength to dream big, or believe they were whole, capable, and breathtakingly worthy.

When all hope seemed lost, I borrowed belief from women who'd turned grit into glitter. I cheered their red-carpet moments like they were mine.

Women who made their first million in under two years, women who came from nothing and built a fortune out of thin air. Yet, they remained humble, down-to-earth, and honest, keeping their sense of humor when they made mistakes and talking to their audience like they truly mattered. These women didn't just build empires; they built lives that once felt out of reach to me. They provided for their families in ways I could only dream of, proving

anything is possible when you take charge of your life.

It wasn't the expensive handbags or jewelry that caught my eye. No, what I envied was their freedom – the ability to travel, make choices without second-guessing, and live life unapologetically on their terms. That's what I craved. I didn't just want financial freedom; I needed it. For my girls, for myself, for the freedom to say, "Price tag? What price tag?" and provide experiences that would bond us as a family.

If you've seen *The Princess and the Frog*, you'll know that Tiana is one of the few Disney princesses who doesn't need a man to rescue her. She's a symbol of strength, independence, and perseverance. A woman who works tirelessly to turn her dream of owning a restaurant into a reality. (Okay, I don't make my clients work day and night as it's unhealthy and defeats the whole point of freedom—but Tiana didn't have a coach or a choice!) The story is a reminder:

Honoring our dreams and the promises we make to ourselves.

And yet, many of us still grow up with the tale of a prince sweeping in to save the day and take care of everything. Why is that even a narrative we are expected to entertain? It's time to rip that storybook to shreds because wishing upon a star doesn't bring happiness. Neither does kissing frogs.

Rip Off the Band-Aid

Waiting for the perfect plan, the perfect timing, and permission is self-sabotage. At some point, you'll realize waiting isn't an option anymore; one day, you'll wake up feeling "Enough is enough!"

Trust me, I know from experience.

One night, after what felt like the millionth round of doubts and fears—"Who am I to do this? What if I fail? What if everyone laughs at me?"—I snapped. Enough. It was time to rip off the band-aid and do what I felt called to do, *unapologetically*.

I went inward and turned down the noise— other people's opinions, society's doubts, even my inner critic until I hit the truth sitting at the bottom of my heart: I wanted to help women get rich. Not just pay-the-bills rich. Rich-rich. Shamelessly rich. *Swimming-in-money-if-they-want-to* rich.

That's how The Red Heel BO$$ was born. I poured my creativity, love for design, and passion for storytelling into a brand that wasn't just pretty, but powerful. Hitting "publish", I realized every business I've built has been another way to honor the dream I had as a kid.

Back when I played doctor with my plastic kit, I didn't just want to fix scraped knees—I wanted to heal. Now, as a brand visionary and confidence coach, I help women rewrite their stories, build their dreams, and reclaim their power.

I collapsed into bed that night —spent and exhilarated—and woke up viral. Messages poured in: "I love your brand!" "I love what you stand for!" "Your content energizes me!" "I love the red heels!"

The thing I'd been too scared to do became the thing that changed everything.

The Business of Being Present: Naptime CEO

I was never built to line up for the old script: climb the ladder, collect a title, take one vacation, collapse. If the highlight of your year is sleeping through a beach trip just to survive your manager's "I'm hilarious" jokes and the resident know-it-all's unsolicited TED Talks... is that success?

Real success is personal.

→ It's **time** freedom to be with your people (or with yourself).

→ It's **energy** freedom to create what lights you up.

→ It's **location** freedom to work from Bali, the couch, or both.

For me, success looked like being there for my girls from the time they were tiny.

It looked like organizing festivals while they napped, so I could do what really mattered when they were awake. It looked like showing up for every school trip, reading picture books to a circle of cross-legged first-graders, and hot-gluing sequins onto costumes the night before a class production because, of course, the tutu needed "more sparkle."

It looked like perching on the edge of the pool for every swimming lesson and clapping through cartwheels at gymnastics; like playdates with flour-dusted noses after we baked, cooked, and made a glorious mess together. I taught them to thread a needle and run a seam straight-ish; we covered the dining table in paper, paint, and dreams.

It looked like being there when they were sick—making soup from scratch, rubbing little backs, turning the lights low, and rearranging work without asking anyone's permission.

It looked like feeding them well because I had the time to chop the veggies and the money to choose the good stuff.

It looked like watching them flourish, and being the soft place they fell when they were hurt or scared.

It looked like earning well enough to show them what's possible: booking holidays when we felt like it, driving to the pool on a Tuesday just because the sun was out, saying yes to Disney on Ice and spontaneous movie nights, then singing our hearts out to the Frozen soundtrack in the car on the way home. "Let it grow, let it grow!" (Yes, it was 'grow' for us!)

That—*that*—is financial freedom. The quiet, everyday privilege of choosing where, how and with whom you spend your hours, your energy, your presence. Not every moment is measured by money, but so many are made possible by it.

And yes—my girls already get it. They're not dreaming of clock-ins; they're dreaming of living. They've seen that "good money comes only from hard suffering" is a myth. Money is energy. It flows where it's welcomed and used with purpose. It buys the most precious thing we have: **choices**.

Warning! When switching to entrepreneurship, it's easy to trade a 9-to-5 for a 24/7. I get it, you are passionate and you care.

The goal isn't to hustle yourself into another cage with nicer wallpaper but to learn how to run a profitable business that supports your life, not the other way around.

When you are clear on your mission, show up authentically, set boundaries, and build systems that work for you, you can fall into the rhythm of your life. Whether success means sipping on a cocktail in the Bahamas, soaking in the spa, or cheering your kid at the soccer tournament, you can be more present and at ease. As money makes those choices possible, again and again.

The power of a personal brand is to be your magnet that brings clients and income as much as freedom, happiness, and fulfillment.

The Heart-Driven Advantage

Women aren't one-note. We're multi-passionate, creative, and connection-driven. That's a *strength, not a problem*. A personal brand lets you bring your whole self to the table with all the variables and build a business that *expands with you as you evolve and change*.

Where many women get stuck: trying to build a brand that "fits the market" before it fits *themselves*. That's backwards. Inside-out branding (how we do it at The Red Heel BO$$) starts with who you are, then decides what you sell.

Inside-out in action (quick snapshots):

→ **The "five worlds" founder:** cyber security + personal development + yoga + long-distance running + cloud storage. On paper, chaos. Under the hood, one golden thread: protecting, strengthening, and freeing what matters. Building a brand that grows with the founder, not against them.

→ **The spiritual coach who was told to "pick one":** boxing herself into a tiny niche killed her fire. We kept all her gifts alive, then chose one or two to *lead with* from the place of *passion and connection*. Her message got clear, her energy came back, and clients knew exactly why she was the one.

Why this works (and keeps working):

→ **Clarity without shrinking.** Lead with your strongest hook, keep the rest in orbit.

→ **Magnetism, not convincing.** When your brand matches your insides, your audience feels it and leans in.

→ **Built-in flexibility.** Pivot, add revenue streams, or reinvent—without starting from zero.

Bottom line: you don't have to choose between your interests. You weave them. A well-crafted personal brand turns your life's mix—skills, stories, scars, and strengths—into a platform for impact, income, and freedom.

Your brand is how your truth becomes tangible. Built from the inside out, it attracts without chasing trends—and it creates a ripple of positive change. When you're well-resourced, money moves into paychecks for freelancers, stability of teams, oxygen for causes, care for family, and mentorship for the next woman up. The more in your hands, the more you can share.

Pause & Reflect

Your brand essence snapshot.

Goal: be able to *say* your vision and mission clearly enough that a stranger gets it and something that makes you feel proud.

→ **Vision (the world you're building):**
"I'm creating a world where **[who]** can **[do/become]** without **[pain/constraint]**."

→ **Mission (what you do to make it real):**
"I help **[who]** **[achieve result]** by **[your method/edge]**."

Example:

Vision: "A world where women build wealth without apology."

Mission: "I help women turn their story into a brand that funds their freedom."

Three quick prompts to sharpen it:

→ Who am I here for—specifically? (Name the person, not "everyone.")

→ What changes for them because of me? (Feeling + result.)

→ How should doing this feel—for me and for them? (Pick 2–3 words: calm, bold, playful, grounded.)

Tiny truth test:

If your lines don't make you a little braver, they're not done. Add one bolder word (e.g., from "help" to "lead," from "okay" to "extraordinary").

Closing Thoughts

Your brand is the foundation of your business—and your freedom. When who you are on the inside matches how you show up on the outside, selling feels like serving and revenue becomes the by-product of alignment.

Build from your truth. Lead with your gifts. Let your brand do the heavy lifting—so you can live with spaciousness, joy, and choice.

Your Companion for Change

Your last pause.

Have you been on the fence? It's worth it, I promise! Grab your **beautiful companion workbook now.**

The matching pages for Part 4 are created to

guide you to truly live this transformation.

https://www.theredheelboss.com/womanizerworkbook

(or simply scan the QR Code in the image above)

Unapologetic

This might be the end of the book, but it's only the beginning of what's possible for you.

Your Riches, Your Rules

The moment you stop performing, pleasing, and pretending, the mask begins to slip.

You don't just *wake up one day* confident. You build it—moment by moment, choice by choice.

Peeling off that mask isn't easy.

It means facing the fear, self-doubt, guilt, and pressure to "be nice" and not to rock the boat.

But every time you choose to show up anyway, something shifts. You stop shrinking to fit and start expanding to lead.

And with every bold decision, you get clearer, stronger, braver, and more unapologetically *you*.

The **"I've had enough"** moment is the turning point.

Enough of playing small. Enough of putting everyone else first. Enough of second-guessing what you already know deep down.

That's emotional independence. Not perfection. Not toxic positivity. It is radical honesty and ownership of your story and your standards.

And once the mask is gone?

You aren't just free.

You're finally home.

You are *ready* to build, lead, and live.

Build from the love you give yourself—the kind of love that makes you unstoppable. Unstoppable in honoring your dreams, your desires, your freedom. Unstoppable in standing tall in your values, doing it scared, against the odds, just doing it anyway. That love changes everything.

This book isn't about becoming someone new. It's about remembering who you already are: a woman capable of building her own dreams, standing tall in a world that still clings to outdated rules, and rewriting the script for those who come after her.

You've stepped into your power. You've claimed your worth. You've stopped surviving and started shaping your future, on your terms.

So let this be your reminder:

The woman you've been working toward throughout these pages?

She's real. She's here. And she's only just getting started.

It's not your fault you were taught to shrink, stay quiet, or put everyone else first. But it *is* your responsibility to rise now. To claim the space, the voice, and the wealth that have always been yours.

You don't have to follow outdated rules. You don't have to let imposter syndrome run the show.

And you definitely don't have to figure it all out alone.

This is your invitation to dream bigger, live louder, and lead unapologetically. To stand shoulder-to-shoulder with other women rewriting the script, building lives of freedom, love, and legacy.

So grab your favorite green juice (or cocktail—no judgment), put on your boldest heels, and step into the world like you own it.

Because you do.

You are unstoppable.
You are abundant.
You are home.
And above all...

You are unstoppable, unlimited, and utterly unapologetic.

From Story to Legacy

The Red Heel BOSS (TRHB)

TRHB was born from fire and passion, a mission to support women globally to become the best version of themselves and create a life they truly love.

It's designed as a space where women can **expand, create, and rise** both in business and in life.

Running a successful business requires more than strategy. It takes **clarity, confidence, and consistency**. It takes the right **mindset and alignment**, as much as it takes being **heart-centered and purpose-driven.**

When all of this comes together—**feminine energy, aligned strategy, and inner power**—your life and business grow and become magnetic.

TRHB is about building powerful brands from the inside out—weaving your **story, your voice, and your mission** into something unforgettable.

How We Can Help You

We're always looking for women who are ready to own their voice, create demand, and lead with confidence—because when one woman rises, she lifts the rest.

This is your time to **build, lead, and thrive.**

Ready to rise with The Red Heel BOSS?

👠 The Red Heel BO$$ was built for ambitious women who are done playing small and ready to build brands, businesses, and lives they love.

Whether you want to:

- Anchor into a **sisterhood** that elevates you (**Feminine Energy & Business Mastery**)
- Become **certified** and build an iconic brand with unstoppable confidence
- Dive deep with bold breakthroughs in our **Unapologetic Masterminds**
- Or hand it over and let our **Genius Marketing Agency** craft and run it for you…

There's a space here waiting with your name on it.

Ready to rise even higher? Step into your next chapter here:
www.theredheelboss.com/femininemastery

About Annamaria

When Annamaria isn't busy empowering female entrepreneurs through her **coaching business**, creating iconic brands for heart-centered service providers with her Genius Marketing **Agency**, or helping clients increase profit and clarity through her **Business Boost Advisory,** she's already dreaming up or building the next big thing. Whether it's writing a book, launching a new program, or designing services that take women even further, she's always creating with purpose.

Beyond business, you'll often find her at the gym, enjoying movie nights with her daughters, or soaking up the sun paddleboarding on the water. Travel, beaches, and sunshine fuel her soul—because life is meant to be fully lived.

https://calendly.com/trhb/coffee-chat

 # Thank You

To write this book has been the most raw, rewarding, and revealing journey of my life—and I didn't walk it alone. Just like with any significant transformation, it took an *army of support*—professionals who guided me, family and friends overseas and back home who lifted me, and the women who stood beside me, reminding me why this story had to be told.

To my daughters—you are my greatest teachers, my fiercest motivation, and the reason I show up with purpose every day. I know it's not always easy being the daughter of a woman who lives so out loud. I promise I'm still figuring it out, too. But everything I do, I do with you in mind, with love in my heart, and with the hope that one day, this book becomes part of your story too.

To my family who are still here or long gone—you've spent valuable time with me at different phases of my life, showing me beauty in laughter and in challenges, and most importantly, teaching me the complexities and significance of relationships. I cherish my memories with you that captured my heart.

To the friends who became family—thank you for holding space for me through breakdowns, breakthroughs, and everything in between, including my crooked dance moves, tears, and sense of humour. For celebrating my growth and achievements. You reminded me I could be both strong and supported, bold and soft. I couldn't have done this without you.

To my clients, community, and rebel sisters—you've seen me, cheered me on, and shared your own stories with vulnerability and strength. You gave me the inspiration to tell mine. Your transformation is the living proof that this work matters. I am endlessly inspired by you.

To the men who lead with heart—uplifting without ego and honoring a woman's brilliance because of her power, not despite it. From my dad and grandfathers, to my physio, my NZ family, and the closest friends who've shown me constant strength and loyalty. *This world needs more of you.*

To those who challenged me, stretched me, and unknowingly helped me grow—thank you for the powerful lessons in self-respect, boundaries, and resilience. Every 'no' I learned to say, every moment that tested my strength, helped shape the woman writing these words today. My worth was never up for debate—and now, I live like I believe it.

To my editor and publishing team—your support, belief, and patience meant the world. Thank you for guiding this vision from draft to masterpiece, for polishing my voice without dimming it, and for understanding that this wasn't just a book but a rebirth. I appreciate you all for holding space for my story with such care.

To my teammates—who keep everything moving both behind the scenes and on the storefront, even when life and family commitments pull me away. You create everything as a true reflection of my brand, vision, mission, and heart. It's everything I ever wished for in an internal TRHB family—a connection deeper than work. Your beautiful commitment and loyalty mean the world to me.

To the mentors, teachers, and thought-leaders—some of you I've met in person, others I've only known through books, podcasts, or online programs—but each of you has shaped my journey in a powerful way. Thank you for showing me what's possible, for expanding my mindset, and for helping me become the woman, mother, and CEO I am today.

To the professionals who help me keep it all together—thank you for seeing me as a whole person, not just the little pieces. From the beauticians who keep me glowing, to my orthodontist and hygienist who gift me a confident smile, to my personal trainer who pushes me stronger, my spiritual guide who grounds me, and my business mentor who lifts me higher.

To my business partners & work family who never cease supporting me—you play a part in elevating me, inside and out. You believe in my abilities even when I don't. You are always by my side, celebrating the wins and going with the flow when things get harder.

And lastly, **to the reader holding this book**—thank you for meeting me here. You didn't stumble across these pages by accident. Something brought you here—maybe a sign, a longing, a spark. I hope it reminds you of your own power.

And if Negative Nancy ever tries to drag you down, remember—she only has the power you give her. Tell her, "Thanks, but no thanks." Show her who is in charge of your story, who can rise into a confident, whole, and unapologetic woman. When she says, "You can't", remind her that you already have—by being here, by choosing yourself, by turning this page.

Here's to the journey of becoming whole.
Here's to telling the truth, even when it's hard.
Here's to you, beautiful rebel. This is just the beginning.

More is coming: books on manifestation and money mindset, body and self-love, attraction marketing, sustainable business models, sales without selling, and building magnetic brands.

Each one will peel back another layer, go deeper, and help more women come home to themselves.

Thank you for walking this chapter with me.

P.S. If this book sparked something in you—an idea, a memory, a story of your own—I'd *love* to hear it.

Your voice, your journey, and your wisdom matter.

Reach out and share your story, or let me know what you'd love to read or learn about next.

Whether it's a topic you want me to write about, speak on, or teach in a program—I'm all ears (and red heels).

Let's stay connected: hello@theredheelboss.com

@theredheelboss on (nearly) all social media platforms!

Resources

Bruckner, M., & DeCamp, M. (2023). The societal value of women-led businesses. Ernst & Young LLP. https://www.ey.com/en_us/entrepreneurial-winning-women/study-on-the-societal-value-of-women-led-businesses

Global Entrepreneurship Monitor. (2023). Women's entrepreneurship 2021/2022: Thriving through crisis. https://www.gemconsortium.org/reports/womens-entrepreneurship

National Women's Business Council. (2022). Annual report: By the numbers. https://www.nwbc.gov/annual-reports/2022/index.html

Weltman, B. (2024). State of women-owned businesses in 2024. Big Ideas for Small Business. https://bigideasforsmallbusiness.com/state-of-women-owned-businesses-in-2024/

Wikipedia contributors. (2024, August 6). Tory Burch. Wikipedia. https://en.wikipedia.org/wiki/Tory_Burch

About the Author

Annamaria is a rebel brand visionary, business mentor, and unapologetic voice for women who are ready to stop shrinking and start owning their brilliance. After breaking free from relationships that no longer served her, she rebuilt her life, identity, and businesses from the inside out — all while raising her two daughters, now blossoming into young adults.

Originally from Europe and now living in New Zealand, Annamaria has spent half her life on each side of the world, blending culture, resilience, and freedom into everything she does. With over 18 years of entrepreneurial experience, she helps female founders claim emotional independence and financial freedom through personal branding, mindset mastery, and feminine-led strategy. Her signature brand, *The Red Heel BO$$*, empowers women to rise as leaders, make money with meaning, and live life on their terms—unfiltered, unchained, and unstoppable.

When she's not mentoring clients or building empires, you'll find her building her mind, body, and soul by workouts, paddleboarding, swimming, soaking in the sun, or out enjoying good food, music, and meaningful conversations. She's passionate about self-discovery, holistic health, spiritual intelligence, and proving that life is best lived in balance — with room for a little spice and a lot of soul.

Through the NAKED! series, she leads women through the powerful process of shedding the old — conditioning, self-doubt, toxic cycles — and coming home to their raw, real, and rebel selves.